Introduction

Have you ever created a great perfume, one that everybody loved, but you could never make it again because you couldn't remember how you made it? You did it with some essential oils and other aromatics but you can't remember what they were or where you got them. Tragedy.

With the formula in your hands, today you might be making money with that perfume and possibly others that you've made over the years. But – pity! – they are all lost forever because you never took the simple steps that would have made them immortal. *You never recorded the formulas!*

It's so simple

A perfume formula is nothing more than a piece of paper with a few lines on it. Some formulas are worth millions of dollars. Yours could be worth... something.

What you might find surprising is that a perfume formula is more like a recipe in a cookbook than a page out of a physics textbook. A perfume formula is easy to understand. It just shows you how to repeat what you did when you created your perfume.

And there's more

With an accurate formula in your hands you can license others to produce your perfume (they might be really good marketers who can bring in money for you!)

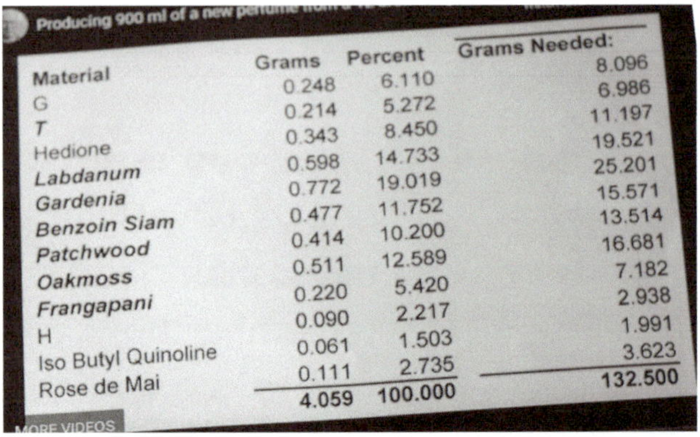

Producing 900 ml of a new perfume

Material	Grams	Percent	Grams Needed:
G	0.248	6.110	8.096
T	0.214	5.272	6.986
Hedione	0.343	8.450	11.197
Labdanum	0.598	14.733	19.521
Gardenia	0.772	19.019	25.201
Benzoin Siam	0.477	11.752	15.571
Patchwood	0.414	10.200	13.514
Oakmoss	0.511	12.589	16.681
Frangapani	0.220	5.420	7.182
H	0.090	2.217	2.938
Iso Butyl Quinoline	0.061	1.503	1.991
Rose de Mai	0.111	2.735	3.623
	4.059	100.000	132.500

This is a perfume formula for one of my fragrances. Notice how several materials have coded designations so I'm not giving it all away. This is a screen shot from a YouTube video.

But that's all in the future. Your first step is to start recording your formulas, to make them immortal! The pages that follow show you how to do it.

If you want to test the commercial power of one or more of the perfumers you've made, *become a formula writer*. As you create a perfume, write down how you created it. What essential oils or other aromatics did you use? How much of each did you use? If you capture this simple information while you are creating, you are only a few steps away from producing a written formula that *could* become a money maker for you.

The pages that follow guide you through the steps that turn the record you made of your perfume's creation into a professional perfume formula.

Chapter 1
First steps toward writing a professional formula for your own perfume

It's all about record keeping and when you're creating a fragrance, record keeping is not difficult. You just have to train yourself to do it. It simply means that, while you are sniffing your way through a new creation, you need to keep a pen and notebook handy. You need to write down all the important stuff. It's not hard. You just have to know

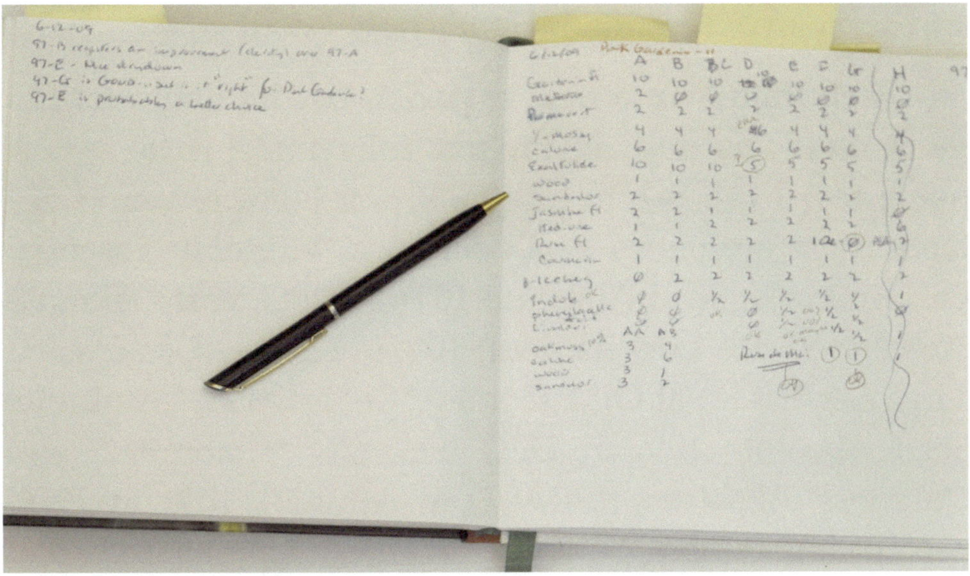

This is a notebook I used while developing several fragrances. Train yourself to write down every trial you make. If you leave out important information you'll be kicking yourself when you hit a winner and are missing some of the details on how it was made.

what to record.

The records you need to keep while creating your perfume are (1) a list of every material used, (2) the amount of each material used, and (3) the identity and *source* of every material you use. With this information you can produce an accurate formula. None of this is complicated. It only requires you to keep your pen and notebook handy while you are creating.

1 List everything that went into your perfume

When you are developing your perfume write down the name of every item you use as you use it. As you adjust your fragrance some items on your list are likely to be crossed off (but just cross them off, don't erase them) and some may be added. Here's how I do it

Each time I try a new material, I write down its full name on my list and, next to that full name, I write a short name that I can use in my daily notes. For example, if I have three aromatics — Cedarwood Virginian Essential Oil, Ambrette Seed Absolute 10% in DPG, and Oakmoss Absolute (IFRA Low Atranol) 10% in DPG — Cedarwood Virginian Essential Oil becomes "Cedarwood," Ambrette Seed Absolute 10% in DPG becomes "Ambrette," and Oakmoss Absolute (IFRA Low Atranol) 10% in DPG becomes "Oakmoss." But always keep a separate record of the *full* description of the material your short name refers to.

These short names will do fine as long as you don't add any conflicting items. For example, if I started to use Ambrette Seed Absolute 1% in DPG while I was using "Abbrette" to denote Ambrette Seed Absolute 10% in DPG, I might revise my short name for it and call it "Ambrette-10" while giving Ambrette Seed Absolute 1% in DPG the short name "Ambrette-1".

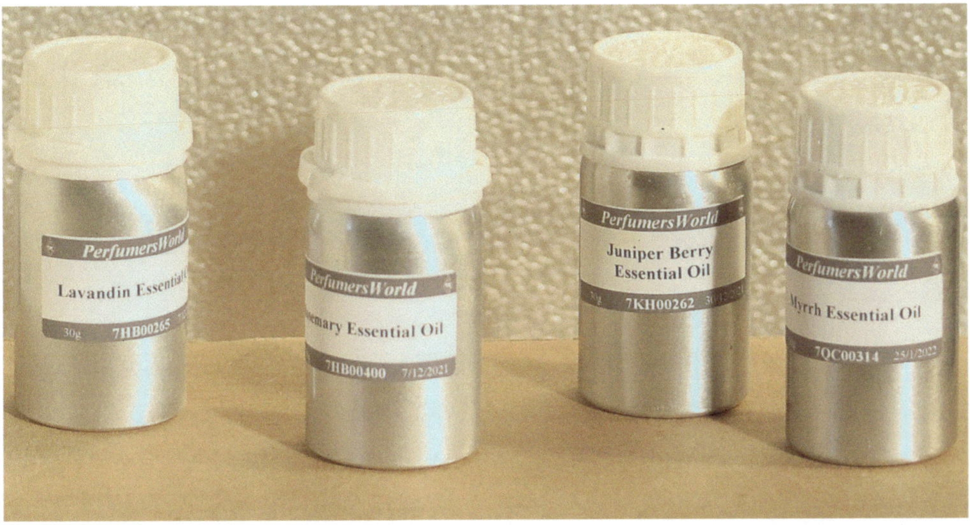

Here are some materials I used for a project. Their full descriptions are: "Lavandin Essential Oil, PerfumersWorld, Code 7HB00256, 7/12/2021," Rosemary Essential Oil, PerfumersWorld, Code 7HB00400, 7/12/2021," Juniper Berry Essential Oil, PerfumersWorld, Code 7KH00262, 7/12/2021," and "Myrrh Essential Oil, PerfumersWorld, Code 7QC00314, 7/12/2021." These descriptions identify the product, the source (PerfumersWorld), the vendor's code, and the date these small cans were filled by the vendor. In my daily notes I used the short names "Lavandin," "Rosemary," "Juniper," and "Myrrh."

Note:

DPG is the common abbreviation for Dipropylene Glycol, a nearly odorless solvent used to reduce the strength of odorants. "Ambrette Seed Absolute 10% in DPG" would indicate that the oil is 10% Ambrette Seed Absolute and 90% DPG. Using Ambrette Seed Absolute at 10% would give you quite different results than using Ambrette Seed Absolute at full strength.

"Oakmoss Absolute (IFRA Low Atranol)" indicates that this Oakmoss has been processed to IFRA (The International Fragrance Association) standards to reduce irritants.

Short names are useful because they save time when taking notes. When I'm working on a fragrance I'm always a bit rushed, eager to discover the effect of new materials and new combinations of materials. Yet I want to maintain an accurate record of each new material and each new combination I try. If I had to write down the full name each time I used an ingredient I would probably get sloppy and in time my notes would become less accurate. Using short names in my notes is a way to maintain their accuracy.

2 Record the amount of each material you used

Here comes the first technical issue. You must record the *amount* of each material used but how can you do it? How can you make accurate measurements? A global fragrance company may measure ingredients by weight. For them in making a trial some ingredients will be used in a very small weights but *they* have the equipment needed to measure very small weights. *Their* equipment costs tens of thousands of dollars. What *they* use to make measurements is of no help to you.

If you can't accurately weigh the small amounts of material you are using could you possibly measure them by volume? Here again you run into the problem of not having the equipment needed to accurately measure fractions of a fluid ounce or milliliter. But you *can do* exactly what many perfume developers do. You can take your measurements in *drops* squeezed out of dropper bottles.

Working with dropper bottles

For creators of perfume who do not have access to a sophisticated laboratory (and that includes most of us), developing a new fragrance by counting out drops from dropper bottles is a standard technique. Dropper bottles allow you to work with reasonable accuracy with small quantities of material. This is important because some materials you might want to use – certain essential oils for example – can be quite expensive. You will want to limit the amounts used in your experiments, your "trials" as they are called. But to get the most accurate measurements possible with dropper bottles there are guidelines to follow.

Rule # 1 — All your bottles and droppers should be the same size and come from the same source. Some of the materials you purchase may come in small bottles without droppers, some may come in small dropper bottles, others may come in large dropper bottles. Since your goal is for all drops to be as equal in size as possible, your droppers and dropper bottles themselves should be uniform in size and newness. You can achieve

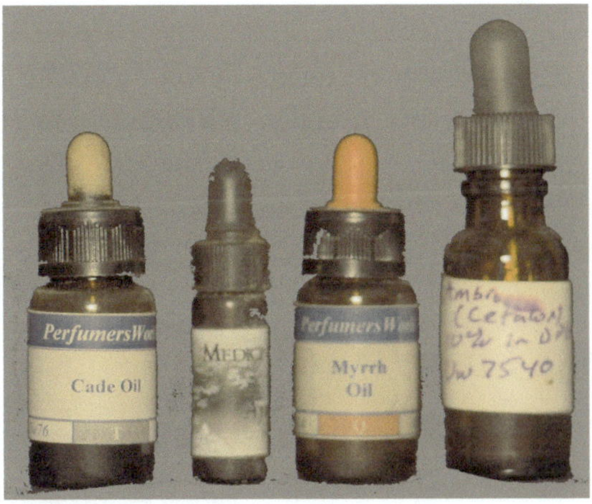

Notice how these bottles differ in size. Drops from their droppers will also differ in size. Notice also that the dropper on the left is discolored from age. Although it is the same size as the dropper second from right (Myrrh) its drops may be irregular in size. Your goal when using dropper bottles is for all the drops to be as close to the same size as possible.

One way to insure that all your drops are close to the same size is to put your aroma materials in new dropper bottles with new droppers.

this by purchasing a quantity of bottles with matching eyedroppers and then transferring your materials to these bottles. Then not only will the glass tubes of the droppers be uniform but the rubber bulbs will all have close to the same resistance when squeezed.

HINT: be sure to label each dropper bottle carefully with what you have put in it.

Rule # 2 — As your goal is to make the drops from your dropper bottles as uniform in size as possible, make it a habit to hold your droppers in the same position when squeezing out drops. Some say the droppers should always be held straight up. I have found that for some thin, runny materials this allows unwanted drops to drip from your dropper throwing off your count. I personally hold my droppers at about a 45 degree angle. This helps

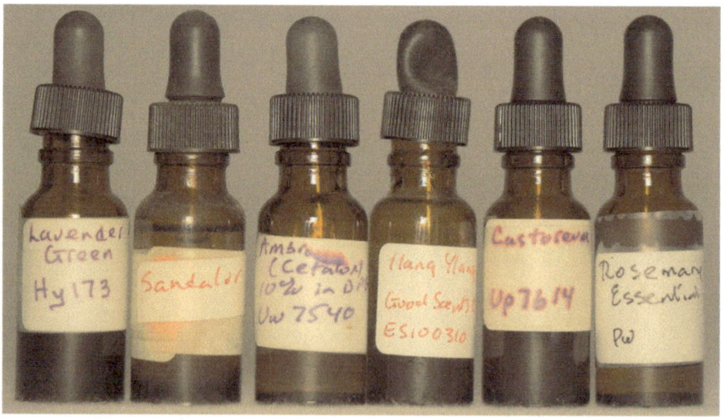

When you transfer materials to new bottles be sure to label them. Notice here the bottle third from the right. The bulb of the dropper is distorted and the dropper should be replaced with a new one. The bottle itself is fine.

prevent those extra drops from escaping on their own.

I was taught that half drops can be achieved by slowly releasing a bit of material onto a toothpick and allowing less than a full drop to fall into my container. Another trick for which accuracy can't be guaranteed is, when you want the smallest amount possible of a material, just wet the tip of a toothpick and then stir it into your mixture. This might be considered 1/1000th of a drop and, while the technique has some merit, it doesn't lend itself to careful record keeping. However, if you ever get a chance to inspect a formula by a professional perfumer, you may see certain materials being used in seemingly microscopic amounts. Personally I try to avoid working with anything smaller than half a drop unless I'm creating a small trial for my own pleasure.

Rule # 3 — Record the source and identity of every material you use. The issue is *continuity*. To *make* more of the same you have to be able to *buy* more of the same. When shopping for materials always ask yourself, "Will I be able to get more of it?"

You are most likely to be able to get more of the materials you are using if you buy them from established sources that continue to offer them year after year. For synthetic materials look for CAS numbers. They are precise identifiers.

CAS numbers

The *Chemical Abstract Service*, founded in 1907 and

now known as the *CAS Registry*, assigns numbers to chemical compounds "that have been described in literature." For you the significance of CAS numbers is that they are a way to communicate the identity of aroma materials to a third party.

Essential oils generally will *not* have CAS numbers since by their nature they are imprecise blendings of multiple chemicals and can differ greatly from one batch to the next depending on how they were processed, where the material was harvested, and even the season and year in which the material was harvested.

Vendors that serve major fragrance houses try to iron out inconsistencies between batches of essential oils produced in different years or seasons by carefully blending them.

Your best hope for consistency is to buy from a vendor that serves commercial fragrance houses.

For materials without a CAS number, your records should identity them by vendor's name, the aroma material's name, and the vendors stock or catalog number.

A particularly important issue with continuity occurs when you have a third party producing your perfume. You don't have to be a big company to have your perfume produced by third party professionals. Many of my fragrances have, after I signed off on a small sample, been produced by for me by a third party, using one of my formulas. But to produce your fragrances successfully, along with your formula you have to give the production team the *exact* identity of the materials you have used so they can find the same.

Problems to look out for

I have a variety of essential oils on hand that I have been given as samples or purchased out of curiosity to sample a particular aroma. None of them will ever be used in a perfume I create. Why? Simply because I can't be sure exactly what they are and I can't be sure I can get more of the exact same. When you buy the aroma materials you are going to work with, give some thought to their source. Your best bet is to buy off a well respected website, one that has been around for a number of years, one that has

Holding the dropper vertical is a recommended practice. In my opinion this does not work well with thin, runny materials.

I like to hold my droppers at an angle as, from my experience, thin, runny materials are less likely to add unwanted drops. Whichever way you choose to hold your droppers, be sure to hold them in the same position for all your drops from all your bottles.

been recommended by others, and one that gives you solid information about their products.

Avoid oils sold in health food stores unless they are from a very well known brand. In spite of what you read on the label you can't really be sure of what you are getting, especially when you are buying a blended oil. How much ingredient "A" does it contain? How much of ingredient "B"? Will the ratio be consistent?

Beware of essential oils advertised as authentic but are being sold at too low a price. You may get a little of what is advertised on the label but you might get more of other things along with it and you can't be sure of what they are.

Chapter 2

Writing your formula in drops prior to weighing it

Written in drops, your formula could look like this:

MATERIAL	**DROPS**
Clove Bud Oil	7
Ambroxan	1
Lyral	2
Benzyl Salicylate	8
Cade Oil	1
Sandalor	12
Ethylene Brassylate	11
Total =	**42 drops**

As written, this formula will produce just 42 drops. Not very much. To produce a larger quantity of this fragrance we could multiply the number of drops of each material by some number, large or small, depending on how much of our perfume oil we wanted to produce. Say we wanted to produce 4,200 drops of our fragrance. Our formula would now look like this:

MATERIAL	**DROPS x 100**
Clove Bud Oil	700 drops
Ambroxan	100 drops
Lyral	200 drops
Benzyl Salicylate	800 drops

Cade Oil	100 drops
Sandalor	1200 drops
Ethylene Brassylate	1100 drops
Total =	**4200 drops**

But look at the tedious work and the intense concentration required to produce this larger quantity – which really isn't so large at all. While we only have to count out 100 drops of Ambroxan and 100 drops of Cade Oil, we will have to count out 1200 drops of Sandalor and 1100 drops of Ethylene Brassylate. It's highly probable that you could loose track of your count somewhere around the 300 drop mark. Then you would have to throw out the drops you have already counted (since you can't be sure of their quantity) and start all over again – and likely you will encounter the same problem again.

Working with percentages

If we knew the percentage of the weight of the finished fragrance each material represented, we would not have to count drops. We would take the weight of the fragrance oil we wanted to produce and then combine the materials in the formula by the percentage of the weight of the formula each material represented. In short, we would have a formula we could use to produce *any* amount of fragrance that we wanted using *any* measurement of weight requested (kilos, pounds, tons, etc.).

For example, if we knew that our fragrance was a mixture of A,B, and C and, by weight, A was 20 percent, B was 37 percent, and C was 43 percent, then to make 10 pounds of the fragrance oil we would simply combine 2 pounds of A, 3.7 pounds of B, and 4.3 pounds of C to give us our 10 pounds. (2 + 3.7 + 4.3 = 10)

Moreover, once this formula was written in percentages of weight it wouldn't matter what unit of measurement we worked with – grams, kilos, ounces, pounds, or even tons. The percentage of each material by weight will be the same.

Converting a formula in drops to a formula in percentages of weight

To convert our formula in drops to a formula in percentages of weight we start by weighing our drops. The weight of any one drop will be too small to measure accurately but if we multiply the number of drops of each material by a number that will allow us an accurate measurement of the *smallest* material, weighing becomes practical.

Multiplying the number of drops in the formula above by 100 would make it practical to measure the weights of Ambroxan and Cade Oil but counting out 1100 drops of Ethylene Brassylate and 1200 drops of Sandalor would be asking for trouble. However if, rather than 100, we multiply each number of drops by 20, 20 drops of Ambrox and and Cade Oil will give us enough weight for accuracy while counting out 220 drops of Ethylene Brassylate and 240 drops of Sandalor are quantities small enough to allow us to keep our focus when counting. Now our formula will look like this and be ready to be weighed using equipment we can afford:

MATERIAL	**DROPS x 20**
Clove Bud Oil	140 drops
Ambroxan	20 drops
Lyral	40 drops
Benzyl Salicylate	160 drops
Cade Oil	20 drops
Sandalor	240 drops
Ethylene Brassylate	220 drops
Total =	**840 drops**

To weigh these drops we will use an electronic balance.

Chapter 3
Introducing the electronic balance

An electronic balance is a tool you can use to weigh the aroma materials used in your perfume. It is, in essence, a scale and not so different than a bathroom scale that weighs people or a kitchen scale that weighs food. Weights of "mass" — the objects being weighed — are displayed digitally. If you are a perfume creator, you may need at least two electronic balances, each with a different

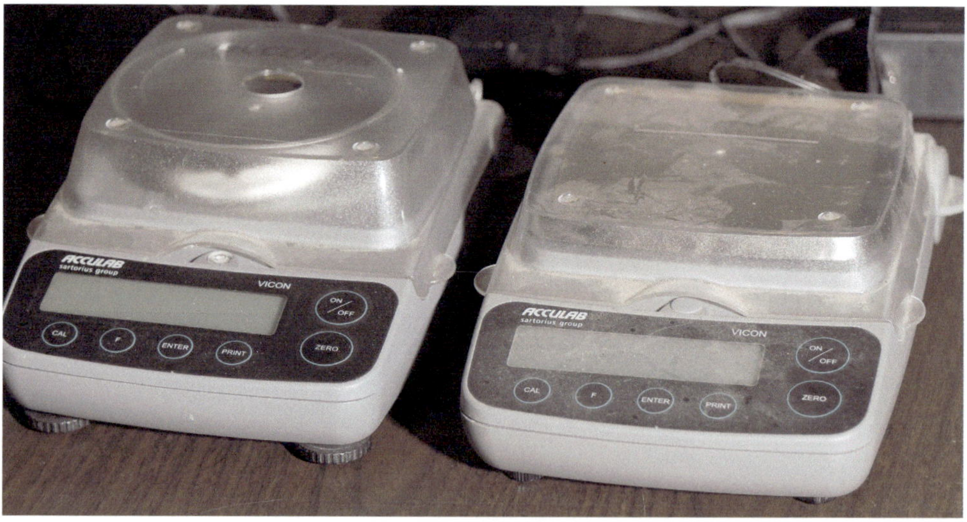

Here are the two electronic balances I use when developing a perfume. The one on the left has 3-digit (0.001) readability and a weighing capacity of 120 grams. The 120 gram capacity is too small for weighing the elements of production batches so I have a second electronic balance (seen on the right) which has a weighing capacity of 3100 grams – but only 1-digit readability (0.1). This model lacks a leveling bubble but an inexpensive leveling bubble from a camera store can do the job.

weighing capacity and different degree of precision.

Purchasing an electronic balance

Cost

As I write this in 2022 you should be able to purchase a good quality electronic balance with all the features you'll need for between $200 and $300. As noted above, you will probably need two of them.

Readability

The first electronic balance you will need is one that will take measurements in grams down to 1/1000th of a gram (0.001 gram) This is referred to as 3-digit (or 3-decimal place) readability. When zeroed the digital display will show 0.000.

Weighing capacity

A balance with 3-digit readability is likely to have a limited weighing capacity. My 3-digit balance has an upper range of just 120 grams. This is not enough for me when I'm producing a perfume. Therefore I also use a balance with a 3100 gram capacity but this balance has only 1-digit readability meaning it will only read down to 1/10th of a gram (0.1 gram) so I can't use it for weighing small quantities. Search as you will, you're not likely to find a single balance that has a large weighing capacity and will weigh down to 1/1000 of a gram.

A/C Adapter

Even when your electronic balance can be powered by batteries, an A/C adapter is almost an essential. No fuss with weak batteries right in the middle of weighing out 100 drops or other inconveniences. Just plug in the adapter, turn on your balance and you're ready to go for as long as your work takes.

Electronic balances in the $200 to $300 price range typically can be powered by batteries. This makes them suitable for field use, away from electric outlets. Most also come with A/C adapters and an A/C adapter is essential (or at least very useful) for laboratory use. For me this is a "must have."

To be leveled (which is essential in weighing), your electronic balance requires four adjustable feet; one of which is shown here. The circle to the left is the door to the compartment where the 100 gram calibration weight is stored.

Adjustable feet and leveling bubble

To get accurate results, your balance has to be leveled. Adjustable feet on the balance are required to level it. When the bubble is centered, your balance is level.

You need to level your balance before weighing anything but some balances are not equipped with leveling bubbles. In this case you can get a leveling bubble (for a camera) from a camera store. Place it in the center of the weighing pan of your balance and adjust the feet of your balance until the bubble is centered.

This is the 100 gram calibration weight for my 3100 gram capacity balance. During the calibration process it is placed in the center of the weighing pan. After use it is stored in a compartment inside the rear of the balance.

Weighing pan

The balance should have a pan on which you will place the objects you are weighing (which will usually be glass containers of some sort.)

Calibration

Your balance will commonly be provided with one or more calibration weights. These are standard weights used when calibrating the balance, an important step

When you move your balance to a new location, or if you haven't used it for a while, it should be recalibrated. This involves placing a calibration weight in the center of the pan of the balance and following the calibration instructions in your user's manual. To the right of the picture you can see the removable pocket in which the calibration weight is stored.

before use. The user's manual for the balance will explain the calibration process.

User's Manual

You should get a user's manual with your balance. This is important and it will explain in greater detail the setup, calibration process and use of your balance. It is also likely to introduce you to capabilities not men-

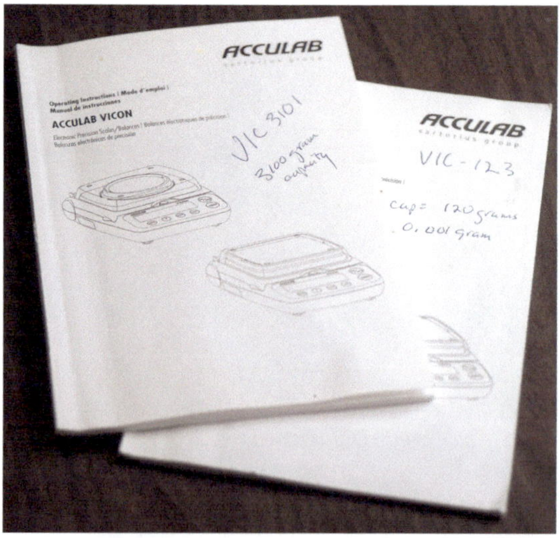

Your electronic balance is a precision instrument and it will give excellent results if used properly. The instruction book that comes with your balance will guide you through the steps to take to achieve accurate results.

The front panel of this electronic balance looks quite simple but there's a lot going on. To the right of the digital readout is the on/off button and below it the button to zero the balance. The smaller buttons from left to right are for calibration (CAL), function (F), enter (ENTER) and print (PRINT). You will make frequent use of the calibration button but perhaps only one-time use of the function button, to select the units of weight you want displaned – grams, ounces, or one of a number of other choices. The ENTER and PRINT buttons would be used only if the balance was connected to an Acculab technical printer.

tioned here. You may never need them but it's nice to know they exist and how you could access them.

How to use an electronic balance

Read the instructions that come with your balance. Set up your balance on a flat, solid surface. Calibrate your bal-

Once your balance is set up and turned on, it is zeroed by pressing the large button at the right. The display will show all zeros and, once it is stable, the small "balance" icon at the left will appear. After about three seconds the readout will begin to drift and the icon will disappear.

The display is showing a weight of 37.232 grams for the flask on the weighing pan of the balance. The "scales" icon is not showing, suggesting that either the display has not yet stabilized or it has already stabilized and then begun to drift.

ance following the instructions in your manual. Be sure that your balance is set to measure the correct weight units (grams, ounces, or something else.)

Start your weighing by zeroing the balance. Place the object to be weighed on the pan of the balance. Wait about three seconds while the display stabilizes. (There may be a symbol in the display that will appear when the display is stable.) Read and record the weight shown in the display. That's all there is to it.

Best practices

The quality of the perfume you produce will depend on the quality of your measurements, both in developing your formula and in producing your finished perfume. Here are some points to be aware of.

Location — Set up your balance on a solid, flat topped table or bench. Avoid setting up your balance on any furniture with a wobble. A heavy table or workbench is ideal.

Environment — Avoid areas of high foot traffic Avoid vibrations from boom boxes, radios, stereos, etc. Keep your balance out of drafts from windows, heating systems, doors, or air conditioners. A draft can throw off your measurements.

Warm up — Allow your balance to warm up before use. Both your balance and the materials you are weighing should be at room temperature. Changes in temperature can affect accuracy.

Contamination — Once you have weighed the container you are using to weight your materials, avoid setting it down on a counter where the bottom of the container may pick up a small amount of unseen debris. For super accuracy (when weighing with a device that goes beyond the 3-digit limit) avoid touching the weighing container with your hands. Use tongs or gloves or a piece of paper wrapped around the measuring container.

Clean up — Clean your balance as soon as you have finished using it.

Moisture — Avoid using your balance in damp areas. Moisture, such as small amounts of condensation, can add small, unwanted weight.

Recalibrate — Recalibrate your balance if it is moved from one location to another.

Room temperature — Early mornings can be cool or hot. Heating and cooling systems may be turned off overnight. By afternoon your laboratory temperature will have adjusted. This is a good time to do your weighing.

Use the center of your weighing pan — Place your weighing container on the center of the pan. If the container is far off center, errors creep in.

More than you really need to know

An electric balance measures the force applied to the pan. That force is converted to an electrical signal and displays on a digital display.

An electronic balance is subject to gravitational pull. Readings can change depending on latitude and altitude which is why repeated calibration is essential.

If your balance fails to stabilize, moisture could be the culprit.

All measurements have some degree of uncertainty. Measuring several times and averaging the results is one way to limit uncertainty.

Analytical balances that measure to four places (0.0001 grams) generally cost from about $1500 to $40,000 or more and require regular professional calibration.

You cannot control all sources of error. Multiple trials and averaging can help control errors, to a degree. The percentage of error you can expect can be calculated mathematically but I can't explain how this is done.

Even an accurate balance will drift after a number of seconds. Note the weight on the display and write it down before your display drifts.

Plastic and glass weighing containers can hold an electric current that can cause inaccuracies in weighing.

Chapter 4

Weighing drops and calculating percentages

Now, using an electronic balance, we can weigh our "drops times 20" formula and then calculate the percentage of the weight that each material in our formula represents.

First we weigh our drops:

MATERIAL	DROPS	WEIGHT IN GRAMS
Clove Bud Oil	140 drops	55.563
Ambroxan	20 drops	16.410
Lyral	40 drops	1.581
Benzyl Salicylate	160 drops	22.200
Cade Oil	20 drops	33.370
Sandalor	240 drops	40.115
Ethylene Brassylate	220 drops	87.313
Total =	**840 drops**	**256.562 grams**

Then we calculate what percentage of the formula those weights represent:

MATERIAL	GRAMS	PERCENT OF FORMULA
Clove Bud Oil	55.563 / 256.562 x 100	= 1.657
Ambroxan	16.410 / 256.562 x 100	= 6.396
Lyral	1.581 / 256.562 x 100	= 0.616

Benzyl Salicyl	22.200 / 256.562 x 100 =	8.653
Cade Oil	33.370 / 256.562 x 100 =	3.001
Sandalor	40.115 / 256.562 x 100 =	15.636
Ethylene Brassylate	87.313 / 256.562 x 100 =	34.032
Total =	**256.562 grams**	**99.991**

A quick review of what we've just done:

First we weighed the drops of each material and recorded the result in grams. Then, to calculate the percentage of the formula (by weight) of each material represented, we divided its weight by the total weight of all the materials (256.562 grams) and then multiplied the (*decimal*) result by 100 to give us the *percentage* of the formula (by weight) that material represented.

The total of all the percentages should come to 100 but numbers had been rounded off, both in weighing and in multiplying. Coming up with a total of 99.991 percent is a good result and we are only slightly off the "100" mark.

And now we can produce any weight of our formula we want

For example, suppose we wanted to produce 15 kilos of our formula. The math would look like this:

MATERIAL	PERCENT	WEIGHT NEEDED
Clove Bud Oil	21.657% of 15 =	3.25 kilos
Ambroxan	6.396% of 15 =	0.96 kilos
Lyral	0.616% of 15 =	0.09 kilos
Benzyl Salicylate	8.653% of 15 =	1.30 kilos
Cade Oil	13.001% of 15 =	1.95 kilos
Sandalor	15.636% of 15 =	2.35 kilos

Ethylene Brassylate		34.032% of 15 =	5.10 kilos
	Total =	**99.991%**	**15.00 kilos**

Quick review of what we've just done

To produce a total of 15 kilos of our formula we calculated the weight each of our materials contributed to the 15 kilo total using the necessary percentage of each material we had already calculated.

The importance of what we have done

By translating our original "drops" formula into a formula of percentages of weight we can now calculate the weight of each material needed to produce this perfume oil in any amount and in any units we choose. ***The formula is now universal.*** Anyone with a copy of this formula and a knowledge of the exact materials required can recreate our fragrance oil simply by combining the materials.

Produce, wait 30 days, and then test it

With your new "by percents" formula in hand I suggest you test its accuracy by making a small batch of your perfume oil, perhaps half a kilo (500 ml). Then, as always when you mix aroma materials, wait 30 days to give them time to blend. Shake them up from time to time while they are blending. At the end of 30 days (or a bit more) sample what you have made by comparing its scent to that of a small sample made from your original "drops" formula. How closely do the scents match?

Ideally you will get a good match. If so, you're on your way to making as much of your perfume oil as you want. But it is also possible that this new batch may be slightly off in one or more notes. Now, with the aid of your nose, you can fix *both* the batch of perfume oil you just made *and* your formula.

You be the judge

Is one note off? Not strong enough or too strong? To fix a note that is not strong enough, one that gets buried in the background scent, add more of it to your finished perfume oil. You might start by adding 5 percent of what is called for in your formula. Then, if needed, add another 5 percent, each time recording the weight of what you added. When this procedure brings the scent up to what was wanted, revise your formula to account for this change. Here is an example of how to do it.

Referring to the sample formula above to make 15 kilos of fragrance oil, say the Ambroxan was too weak and we added 5 percent more (0.14 kilos) and then another 5 percent (0.14 kilos). Now, instead of 0.96 kilos of Ambroxan we have used a total of 1.24 kilos, so the weights of the materials used and our new percentages look like this:

MATERIAL	KILOS	NEW PERCENTAGE OF FORMULA*
Clove Bud Oil	3.25 / 15.28 x 100 =	21.27 %
Ambroxan	1.24 / 15.28 x 100 =	8.12 %
Lyral	0.09 / 15.28 x 100 =	0.59 %
Benzyl Salicylate	1.30 / 15.28 x 100 =	8.51 %

Cade Oil	1.95 / 15.28 x 100 =	12.76 %
Sandalor	2.35 / 15.28 x 100 =	15.38 %
Ethylene Brassylate	5.10 / 15.28 x 100 =	33.38 %
Total =	**15.28 kilos**	**100.01%**

**Numbers have been rounded to 2 decimal places.*

If, on the other hand, one material was too strong, since we could not subtract it from what was already made, we would have to raise the level of all the other materials, little by little, until the correct balance was achieved. Our work could look like this if, referring to our formula again, we found that the Clove Bud Oil was too strong and by raising the levels of all the other ingredients by 5 percent, harmony could be achieved. Then our new formula would look like this:

MATERIAL	**KILOS**	**NEW PERCENTAGE OF THE FORMULA**
Clove Bud Oil	3.25 / 15.60 x 100 =	20.83 %
Ambroxan	1.01 / 15.60 x 100 =	6.47 %
Lyral	0.09 / 15.60 x 100 =	0.58 %
Benzyl Salicylate	1.37 / 15.60 x 100 =	8.78 %
Cade Oil	2.05 / 15.60 x 100 =	13.14 %
Sandalor	2.47 / 15.60 x 100 =	15.83 %
Ethylene Brassylate	5.36 / 15.60 x 100 =	34.36 %
Total =	**15.60 kilos**	**99.99%**

**Numbers have been rounded to 2 decimal places.*

When adjusting the scent you produced remember to record the weight of each material you added so that you can recalculate the percentages of each material used and create a new, more accurate formula. When you have done this, the next time you produce a batch of your fragrance oil the results should be spot on.

Chapter 5
Sometimes complications arise and drops present a problem

You have seen now how a formula originally created in drops can be weighed out in grams and then converted to percentages of weight. This eliminates the necessity of counting out huge numbers of drops as when we weigh, we are only dealing with, at most, a few hundred drops of any particular material. But look at this formula. Notice the problem it presents:

Formula 6
Material A = 60 drops
Material B = 120 drops
Material C = 45 drops
Material D = 3 drops
Material E = 70 drops
Material F = 1 drop
Total = 299 drops

To get a large enough quantity of Material F to weigh accurately, we have to multiply all the quantities by some number. Twenty would be the smallest multiplier I would use as it brings Material F up to 20 drops, enough for accurate weighing. But look now at what happens to Material B: 120 x 20 = 2400 drops. And look what happens to Material E: 70 x 20 = 1400 drops. And Material A: 60 x 20

= 1200 drops. I personally don't trust my hand and my eyes measuring out 1200 drops, 1400 drops, and certainly not 2400 drops. So here I'm going to use a different strategy.

I would not recommend this alternate strategy in most situations but counting out a few thousand drops has no appeal to me. Thus I'm going to make my production formula using a different method. However, I have two warnings for you before *you* use this alternative. First, the drops measured out in your original formula must be as uniform as possible. This means you took care to use the same size bottles and droppers for all your materials and you always held the dropper in the same position when squeezing out drops. Then, for this alternative method, you must have a good enough nose to be able to judge whether this method has given you the same scent as your original "drops" formula and, if it has not, you must have a good enough nose to make any needed adjustments.

So here we go.

Rather than take our percentages from the weight of grams, we'll take our percentages directly from the formula in drops:

Table 2

Material A: 60 drops	60/299 x 100 =	20.07 percent
Material B: 120 drops	120/299 x 100 =	40.13 percent
Material C: 45 drops	45/299 x 100 =	15.05 percent
Material D: 3 drops	3/299 x 100 =	1.00 percent
Material E: 70 drops	70/299 x 100 =	23.41 percent
Material F: 1 drop	1/299 x 100 =	0.33 percent
Total drops = 299	**Total percents = 99.66**	

Now we are ready for production. Since it is just the perfume oil we are producing and, in our finished perfume it may be as little as 7 percent of the mixture (alcohol and water supplying the other 93 percent), we will use our production formula to make just 800 milliliters (0.8 liter) of our perfume oil. Remember, we are now working with *volumes* of liquid rather than weights.

So we now calculate:

FORMULA # 2

Percentage of formula by volume		**Volume required to make 800 ml of fragrance oil**
20.07 percent of Material A =	.2007 x 800 =	160.56 ml
40.13 percent of Material B =	.4013 x 800 =	321.04 ml
15.05 percent of Material C =	.1505 x 800 =	120.40 ml
1.00 percent of Material D =	.01 x 800 =	8.00 ml
23.41 percent of Material E =	.2341 x 800 =	187.28 ml
0.33 percent of Material F =	.0033 x 800 =	2.64 ml
	Total =	**799.92 ml**

Measurement tools needed

To measure by *weight* we used an *electronic balance*. To measure by *volume* we will use *graduated cylinders and a kitchen measuring cup*. This equipment is far less expensive than a single electronic balance. Here are the items you now need to add to your perfume laboratory. They all fall under the category of "glassware."

Essential glassware

4-cup Pyrex glass measuring cup. This is something

you can find in your local supermarket. I have several of them and they get a lot of use. You want one that will measure in both fluid ounces (up to 64 fluid ounces) and milliliters, up to 1000 milliliters (1 liter).

4-cup glass measuring cup showing graduations in fluid ounces

Small measuring column. A graduated measuring column that can measure up to 10 milliliters.

Reverse side of measuring cup showing graduations in milliliters

Medium measuring column. A graduated measuring column that can measure up to 25 milliliters.

Large measuring column. A graduated measuring column that can measure up to 50 milliliters or more.

These measuring columns can often be obtained as a set along with other laboratory glassware. A set will often include calibrated beakers of various sizes and these can be useful as containers when you are developing your perfume.

Now let's make use of this measuring equipment to prepare the 800 ml batch of the formula above. Because this is not a "real" perfume, I won't use "real" materials but you can follow these instructions using colored water.

Here is how you assemble your "fragrance"

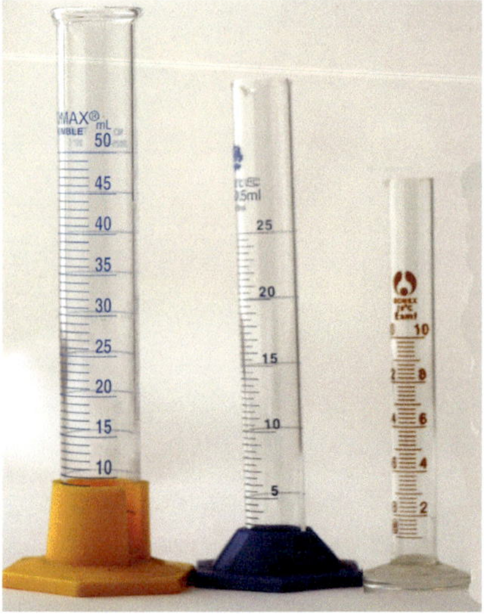

3 measuring cylinders

For Material A you need 160.56 ml so fill you large measuring column to the 50 ml mark three times, each time dumping the contents into your 4-cup measuring cup. This will give you 150 ml. To get your final 10.56 ml use your medium measuring column. Fill it to the 10 ml mark and then add just a little more for the extra half you need. Pour this into your 4-cup measuring cup.

For Material B you need 321.04 ml so fill your large measuring cup to the 50 ml mark six times, each time emptying the contents into your 4-cup measuring cup. Then use your medium measuring cup and fill it to the 21 ml mark. Add the contents to your 4-cup measuring cup.

For Material C you need 120.4 ml so fill your large measuring column to the 50 ml mark twice, each time dumping the contents into the 4-cup measuring cup. Then use your medium measuring column to measure out the additional 20 ml and dump this into the 4-cup measuring cup.

For Material D you need 8 ml so use your small measuring column. Fill it to the 8 ml mark and dump the contents into your 4-cup measuring cup.

For Material E you need 187.28 ml so use your large

measuring column. Fill it to the 50 ml mark three times, each time dumping the contents into your 4-cup measuring cup. Then, again using your large measuring column, fill it to the 37 ml mark and then dump the contents into your 4-cup measuring cup.

For Material F you need 2.64 ml so use your small measuring column filling it slightly above where the 2.6 ml mark would be (if there was one!) Dump the contents into your 4-cup measuring cup.

Now look at the graduations on your 4-cup measuring cup. It should be filled to close to the 798.6 milliliter mark.

If this was real

If you have been mixing real fragrance ingredients instead of colored water, at this point you would have slightly less than 800 milliliters of your fragrance due to rounding errors and small errors in measuring. You would now pour your finished fragrance oil into a bottle, screw on a cap, shake it a bit and let it age for 30 days or more periodically giving it a few shakes.

NOTE: For this I use 1-quart (32 ounce) amber Boston round bottles that come with matching screw-on tops.

But you're not finished yet

The final challenge is to have the patience to wait out your 30 days or a bit longer and then sample what you have made. Here's where you'll need a good nose and some of your original fragrance made by drops. Does the perfume oil in your quart bottle have the same scent as your original composition? Is it, as far as you can tell, a very good match? Or will you need to make some adjustments?

After 30 days
Making corrections

Thirty days after you produced a batch of your perfume oil based on calculations of the volume of your drops it is time to test your results.

You test using your nose. Does the scent of the batch you just made match the scent of your original "drops" formula? Try them both on smelling strips. Are they a good match? If they are not, you'll need to make some corrections.

The good news is that the most likely source of trouble will be materials used in the smallest quantity but before you begin to tinker, be sure that the aroma materials used in your production batch were identical to the materials used in your original batch: same name, same source and, if you have it, same CAS number.

Hopefully your nose is up to sniffing out what, if anything, is not quite right with the fragrance you just produced. If, in fact, it gave you what you wanted or very close to it, stop! There is no sense in messing with success. On the other hand, if what you made is not quite perfect even though you followed your own formula carefully, you'll want to make adjustments. But the questions is, "what isn't quite right?" Which note or notes are not coming through? Or which note or notes are coming on too strong? You are trying to achieve the same balance you had in your original "drops" batch.

At this point it is important to know the scents of the individual materials that went into your perfume and what each one was supposed to do. With this knowledge you can spot the notes that are out of sync and correct them. You may have several notes out of adjustment but let's take the case of a single note that came out too weak. This means you need more of it in your formula and here's a way to achieve that.

NOTE: These adjustments are similar to the adjustments made in Chapter 4 but are measured in volume — milliliters — rather than in grams or ounces.

Suppose after producing 800 ml (or 799.92 ml of Formula # 2 we found Material D wasn't coming through properly and needed to be increased. Five percent of Material D would be 0.4 ml so we would add that to the production batch. And say we needed to add another 0.4 ml to that batch to achieve the scent we were looking for.

Now, rather than having used 8 ml of Material D we have used 8.8 ml. We have corrected the scent of the production batch by adding this extra 0.8 ml of Material D but now we have to correct the formula itself. Here is how we do this:

FORMULA # 3

Material	**Volume used to make 800 ml of fragrance oil**		**New Formula**
Material A =	160.56 ml.	160.56 / 800.72 x 100 =	20.05 %
Material B =	321.04 ml.	221.04 / 800.72 x 100 =	40.09 %
Material C =	120.40 ml.	120.40 / 800.72 x 100 =	15.04 %
Material D =	8.80 ml.	8.80 / 800.72 x 100 =	1.10 %
Material E =	187.28 ml.	187.28 / 800.72 x 100 =	23.39 %
Material F =	2.64 ml.	2.64 / 800.72 x 100 =	0.33 %
			Total = 100 %

If, rather than a note being missing, a note or notes are too prominent, the adjustment requires that you raise the level of the non-offending notes. This can be a bit more complicated, especially if you have used a number of different materials, but it is the only solution. Again you'll need to record exactly what has been added and, when you are satisfied with the scent you have achieved, rework the percentages in your formula to reflect the changes.

Chapter 6
Finishing your perfume by adding alcohol

When you finish your perfume by adding alcohol you find yourself working with volumes. If, for example, you want to produce 40 gallons of perfume at 10 percent fragrance oil to 90 percent alcohol (a common ratio), your volume of oil will simply be four gallons, ten percent of forty.

If you created your formula by percentages of volume, you just do a liters to gallons conversion and you're set to go.

NOTE:
1 liter = .2642 gallons
1 gallon = 3.7843 liters

But what if you followed my recommendation and produced your fragrance by weight? With your formula you can produce any weight of your fragrance oil you need but what weight will give you four gallons? The calculation is not difficult.

First, you need to know the weight of a volume of your fragrance. In this case since we want to produce four gallons of fragrance, we can start by weighing a pint (16

Once you have your formula down, you can have your fragrance produced on a larger scale. The drums seen above are from projects of my own. Notice the red "Flammable" labels that warn of potential fire hazard. These labels are required as the contents of both drums are about 80 percent alcohol. The black drum on the left gave us about 800 2-ounce bottles of a men's cologne. The blue drum gaved us about 1500 1-ounce bottles of a men's cologner. In the case of the black drum, the fragrance was produced for us by a small fragrance house and then sent to a filling house to have the alcohol added. For the blue barrel, the alcohol was provided by the same firm that provided the fragrance. This barrel was a reorder of a fragrance that had sold out. The original supplier, a small company in New Jersey, had been purchased by a major French fragrance house and they provided this new supply for us.

fluid ounces) of the fragrance. There are two pints to a quart and four quarts to a gallon so once we have the weight of one pint of the fragrance we can multiply this weight by eight to get the weight of a gallon. Then, for this example, we multiply the weight of a gallon by four to get the weight of four gallons, which is what is required.

Once you have your formula, whether developed by weights or by volumes, you can produce whatever amount you need. When needed, the math for conversions is very simple. You are now ready to fill a few bottles or to produce your fragrance on an industrial scale.

The truth is that, when you're creating a new fragrance, you can never know in advance how others will react to it. Sometimes, like a new style of music or a new haircut, a new fragrance takes time to catch on – you never know. And that's why you always want to keep a record of what you've done. You want to develop a library of your formulas. Don't loose out on a good payday. Keep that notebook handy while you are creating!

Here are a handful of my own creations. Some were more successful than others but I have the formulas for all of them. As tastes change, some may be set aside; others brought to the front. If you are going to create fragrances, keep creating! And keep those formulas! You never know why or when they may suddenly be in great demand.

Appendix
Where to get stuff

You'll find my major list of sources in the "Vendors" pages of my PerfumeProjects.com website:

http://www.perfumeprojects.com/perfume/vendors/vendor-menu.shtml

Remember, companies are not around forever and, over the years, some of my favorite sources have disappeared. No doubt, in the years to come, more will vanish. But I'll be searching out new ones and they will be listed in those "Vendors" pages.

The important tools for developing production formulas are the electronic balance and glassware. Your sources are the same as those that would supply high school and college chemistry classes. You will find a number of these online. Some ship internationally at reasonable rates. As best I recall, my own balances came from "Affordable Scales and Balances" — http://www.affordablescales.com. They offer both "precision balances" (the category you want) and "analytical balances," balances with 4-digit (0.0001) readability, more sophisticated features, and higher price tags. The models I use are no longer available.

Made in the USA
Las Vegas, NV
03 November 2026

57424061R00031

Youth Justice

&

Youth Offending Teams

Gail Ellis

First published in Great Britain in 2013 by Book Treasury, Cheshire

ISBN: 9781909827011

TABLE OF CONTENTS

ABSTRACT

How effective are the Action Plan Orders, Child Safety Orders, Parenting Orders, Reparation Orders and the Final Warning in reducing offending behaviour? What problems did the Youth Offending Teams encounter with the new legislation under the Criminal Justice Act 1998?

The Criminal Justice Act (1998) brought about significant changes to the Youth Justice System. It aimed to 'nip offending in the bud' by addressing the offending behaviour in order to prevent reoffending.

Youth Offending Teams were to be established and new Orders were to be followed. This book is based on five of those Orders, the Action Plan Order, the Child Safety Order, the Parenting Order, the Reparation Order and the Final Warning.

This book gives an insight into government policies on youth crime, past and present and the role of other non-governmental parties have played in fear of crime, crime and punishment and juvenile justice. It looks at the welfare versus justice debate, a review of previous work, multi-agency partnerships and the results of the pilot studies.

CHAPTER 1

Government Policies on Youth Crime (past and present)

This chapter reflects the view of government policies on youth crime and discusses the intervening ways of those governments and other agencies that have addressed the issues of fear of crime, crime prevention, youth crime and punishment, and considers the effects of those policies to try to determine whether they have been successful.

Government policies on crime prevention have remained in a similar fashion, mainly to punish offenders for their crimes and as deterrence to others. The two philosophies of punishment are *retribution* and *utilitarianism*. Retribution is based on punishment being a moral right and duty for wrong-doing in view of a finding of guilt and utilitarianism has it principles in that the sentence is proportionate to the seriousness of the offence. [1]

Retributivists need only demonstrate that the punishment is deserved. It does not care for the effects that the punishment may have on the offender both now in the present and future, or the effect that it may have on the offender's family. Nor, does it

---

1 Worrall (1997: 11) *Punishment in the Community: The Future of Criminal Justice.*

take into account personal and social factors that led to the offender committing the crime. It does not take into consideration the cost on the government's purse strings.

Utilitarianism is founded on principle that the sentence should fit the crime and basically that no more or less punishment should be given for a certain crime. These principles again do not take other factors into account such as the offender's age, IQ, reasons for committing the offence etc.

Jeremy Bentham (1748-1832) philosopher, jurist and social reformer, argued that utilitarianism has to demonstrate that the punishment or sentence must work and that punishment is itself evil and can only be justified if it brings about a greater good. It does not take into account the relationship between punishment and the seriousness of the crime.

Other non-government organisations have been involved in crime prevention for a long time now. Usually, if organisations are losing money rapidly they invest (at consumers expense through higher insurance policies and higher taxes) to prevent losses which eat away at their profits. Insurance companies are affected by claims from Insurers who make a claim for their losses such as putting in a claim for bikes being stolen from their shed. The fact that the victim is paying directly through insurance and having their insurance premiums raised upon a claim and through taxes for policing and crime prevention suggests that the victim is to blame just as much as the offender for being careless in bringing about the opportunity for a crime to be committed e.g. not securing the shed where the bikes was stolen from. The insurance industry along with the Home Office in the 1950's launched a campaign aimed at the general public and businesses to encourage preventative awareness with a view of easing the financial strain that they were finding themselves under from claims made through, in the main, petty theft.

Getting the message through to communities to prevent crime costs time and therefore money and this job was given to the police who were generally expected to communicate the message of awareness on a local level as part of their statutory duty even though the police lacked the expertise or organisational structure to fulfil the duty. [2]

Police forces usually show their discontent if they are given addition tasks by the government without the extra financial aid to meet the costs as they face policing on a tight budget. The government recognised this so the National Crime Prevention Centre was set up by the Home Office in 1963 in Stafford to provide the police with Crime Prevention training as standard

---

2 Leishmann, Loveday & Savage (1996)

with the central government footing the costs. By 1965 each police force established their own crime prevention department using the recommendations that were contained in the Cornish Report undertaken by the Cornish Committee on the Prevention and Detection of Crime as the old saying goes, *prevention is better than crime.*

Police forces had liaised with officers on the beat to draw up crime prevention survey reports headed by a Superintendent within each police force and a Sergeant would draft up these reports with the required information. Crime prevention was filtering through to the community and Neighbourhood Watch Schemes began which many people were more than willing to take part in as it reduced their chances of members of their household becoming a victim of crime. The police had discussed their concerns with residents in their local community to get them to secure their properties from burglars by fitting window lock burglar alarms and padlocking sheds and other outbuildings. Businesses were given advice as to how to protect their properties from vandalism etc. Open communal spaces were starting to be divided up so those walking about or on bikes could be seen by community members rather than hidden by trees, walls, alleyways and the likes to prevent personal attacks from mugging and bodily harm. With the general public being more aware than ever before it was only natural that more crime would be reported as those in neighbourhood watch schemes would report suspicious people in the area in the hope of preventing a crime in their locality. This observance in communities meant than more young offenders were coming to the attention of the police and the ultimately, the courts.

The media have long played a part in scaremongering a nation into fear in relation to crime amongst other things. With more crime being reported now than ever before, the press would have a field day and the public would be fed a continued diet of persistent criminal acts by youngsters were turning communities and city centres into crime-ridden places. Needless to say many people whether vulnerable or not were becoming fearful of a new generation of young criminals who could wreak havoc on our lives.

To counteract those fears and try to curb crime, the government introduced additional measures to prevent young offenders committing crime, by locking them up. which The objective was two-fold one, by taking the young criminal off the streets and two, reassuring community members that the situation is under control. The Children and Young Persons Act (1969) allowed for and introduced more compulsory measures for local authorities who were given the powers to take over the parental rights of a child and take them into care if they committed criminal offences by the use of 'Care Orders'. The Act itself being would suggest that the blame for these young offenders lay with the parents and as now the government were sending out the message that 'if you can't control your children, then we will',

It was inevitable that more young offenders would be taken into care in the years ahead following this Act. The detrimental effects were that young offenders at a very young age were being locked up for minor, petty offences. This could hardly be said to be taking into the account the principles of utilitarianism that the sentence should fit the crime.

NACRO the children's charity have long sought justice for children. They argue that young offenders between the ages of 10-17 have been at a disadvantage when coming into the criminal justice system. The injustices that have occurred are numerous.

Although the media continually feed us stories of crime – to sell more newspapers, the government also jump on the bandwagon informing us that that they are not going tolerate it anymore and that they are going the extra mile to do more about – usually when an up and coming general election is about to commence.

The fact that the government are also concerned about crime may heighten those fears. Their tactics are influential in helping grab those extra votes to win the election, especially from those who fear crime and a particular Party is willing to do more than the other to prevent it.

The injustices on young offenders were to continue throughout the 1970's under the Labour Party. The fact that more young offenders were being locked up suggested that more serious crime was being committed when in fact, this was not the case; young offenders were being locked up for minor crimes.

This fear of heightened serious crime gave the Conservative Party plenty of ammunition to grab new supporters and helped them win the general election in 1979 after announcing sweeping changes on young offenders. Now young offenders were going to be given a short, sharp shock in a young offender's institute.

Many were already locked up in care homes under the local authority for petty crimes - now it was going to prison! The following table shows the remanding and sentencing of young offenders in penal establishments throughout Europe ten years after the changes. [3]

---

3 NACRO (1989)

Comparison with Other European Countries

Table 1

Number of prisoners per 100,000 population

Luxembourg	103.4
United Kingdom	98.2
Austria	96.0
Finland	93.0
France	92.0
Turkey	90.2
West Germany	86.7
Portugal	84.0
Switzerland	77.6
Belgium	70.5
Spain	69.2
Denmark	69.0
Italy	62.0
Sweden	61.0
Ireland	56.0
Norway	47.0
Greece	42.9
Cyprus	42.0
Iceland	41.3
Holland	36.0
Malta	19.7

The United Kingdom fair very high on the table for adopting harsher penalties on young offenders compared to the rest of Europe. Evidence suggests that this is not because we have more crime than most of Europe but that we are sending our young offenders into the penal system for less serious crimes than our counterparts. Malta has the lowest number of young offenders in prison per 100,000 of the population. Maltese courts may also use a more utilitarianism view and only send young offenders to prison for more serious crimes rather than they have less crime than the rest of Europe per 100,000 of the population.

David Faulkner, Deputy Under-Secretary at the Home Office spoke of crime rates in the UK in 1989 and said:

"The situation in the rest of Western Europe is very much the same as ours – some countries have a bit more burglary or a bit less trouble with minor vehicles, but by and large you cannot say you are better or worse off in France, Holland or Scandinavian countries that you are in England and Wales". [4]

This contradicts the results in the graph which shows that of the young offenders in Denmark only 69.0 are imprisoned, Sweden imprisons 61.0 and Norway 47.0 per 100,000 people.

Hudson (1994) argues that the elaboration of penal policy, which progressed in the 1980's, contained the following features:

A concern to develop clear principles for the assignment of some offenders to prison, some to develop community sanctions;

---

4 (Hudson, (1994: 29)

A desire to base punishment on the seriousness of the offence and/or likelihood of reoffending rather than on the needs or circumstances of the offender;

A concern with rights (formally defined) rather than the remedies-rights of offenders to fair punishment; rights of the public to protection from predatory criminals; rights of the state to retribution and of victims to compensation. [5]

Juvenile justice workers worked with other agencies including the police to try to divert young offenders away from the criminal justice system in the late 1980's to prevent them from getting penal penalties. The police would offer a simple caution to a young offender who had committed a petty crime.

Inter-agency working causing problems itself due to the different previous polices of each organisation. The juvenile worker seeks justice for the child and the police seek justice on behalf of the government.

Blagg (1988) found that *inter-agency working does not necessarily imply that all partners are working towards the same objective.* [6]

---

5 (Hudson (1994: 122)

6 (Haines & Drakeford (1998: 56)

Agencies that are used to working within their own team on using their own principles with the aim of achieving a specific goal suddenly has to work with other agencies such as the police, education and health services that have different principles can cause a *collision* within an inter-agency organisation resulting in disastrous effects. But, surely it is in the interests of criminal justice and crime prevention if a mix of social organisations such as the police, health and social services and such work to establish the cause and health and environmental circumstance of the young offender by addressing the problem, if any, that lies beneath the criminal act.

Politicians from the Conservative Party have continually refused to link criminal behaviour with social problems such as unemployment, poor housing conditions, poverty and addiction. By maintaining the retributivists doctrine and holding the offender responsible solely for his actions and failing to take into account factors that may have caused the young offender to commit the criminal act in the first place, are failing the criminal justice system as a whole.

Rather than the government taking some of the responsibility for the social ills of our society which may be an underling factor of crime, the blame is directed towards the parents of young offenders and that parents should be held responsible as they are the one who should take proper care and control over them. Some would suggest that this is rightly so – we should be solely responsible for ensuring our children are raised in a manner that they will not commit offences, even petty offences.

There were many debates in the media and still continue to this day about the parental responsibilities and youth offending. As more and more offenders are sent to prison and with the media stating that '*we are too soft with our children'* and similar headlines week in week out, the debates will remain.

Haines and Drakeford (1998) agreed that politicians have long identified the parents of young people in trouble as a source of their children's anti-social behaviour.

The White Paper *Young Offenders* (1982) introduced measures to 'reinforce parental responsibility' in control of adolescent family members which were widely attacked by those with sentencing powers and workers in the practice, therefore the powers were being unused. [7]

With more offenders coming before the courts and more of those being sentenced to penal establishments (too many from ethnic minority groups); without any thought as to whether there were any available places to house them.

---

7 Haines and Drakeford (1998)

This led to many young offenders being sent to the other side of the country as there may have been less overcrowding than nearer their homes. This affected the ability for families to visit the offender due to the costs of travel.

The pressure of overcrowding prisons was reaching boiling point as the conditions in the prisons were being affected as cells were being shared, prisons were becoming noisier and dangerous as tensions grew and tempers flared.

This discontent among prisoners resulted in rioting that soon spread in other prisons throughout the country. The Woolf Report followed on from the prison rioting gave rise for cause for concern. Lord Woolf, after reporting on the financial cost duly noted that our prisons were too overcrowded and that many offenders were being sent to prison for minor crimes and/or were sent to prison for too long for their crimes.

The government was forced to act and thus made more changes with the introduction of the Criminal Justice Act (1991). Now sentences were going to be based on a *desert basis* being just with the offence committed. There was to be a distinction between crimes against the person and property crimes to ensure that young offenders would not generally be sent to prison for acts on property which were deemed less serious than criminal acts upon a person.

Community sentences could be given to a young offender where previously they were only given if prison was the alternative sentence.

At last the government had recognised that the maturity of the offending youngster should be taken into account when deciding the sentence. To ease the current overcrowding an offender had an automatic right to be released after serving half of the prison sentence. Previously this had been a right after serving two thirds of a penal sentence. There would be monitoring for discrimination within the criminal justice system to ensure that minority groups and women were not unfairly being sent to prison through closer co-operation with the various organisations within the criminal justice system like the police, probation and the courts. [8]

Despite the government's efforts prisons remained overcrowded which would suggest the courts' were still sending young offenders to be locked up.

Broad (1991) on the Criminal Justice Act 1991 wrote:

So here we go again, on a punishment train with yet more trucks being coupled ... on to an already overburdened and lengthy express, hurtling towards nowhere quickly, with an inexhaustible

---

8 Leishmann, Loveday & Savage (1996: 28)

power supply and seemingly infinite capacity to collect, process and dump its perceived 'human waste' with little thought about the persona, social and environmental costs. [9]

With no end to penal sentencing by the courts this resulted in prisoners being locked up in their cells for up to twenty three hours a day to prevent rioting as prisons could face breaching health and safety rules as the amount of prisoners outgrew the ratio of required staff for health and safety purposes.

Faith in the criminal justice system was showing signs of rapidly deteriorating and numerous press reports and news bulletins were to continually reinforce this. There was hardly any good news with regards to the matters concerning the criminal justice system. Then a killing happened on a small child by two children aged just ten years old which took on a whole new disturbance with regards to future policy and the criminal justice system. With the negativity on our youngsters who commit acts of crime as well as the fear of crime and the state of our nation to allow such a crime to happen by boys still remains to this day.

The killing of James Bulger in 1993, so young was and by two ten year old boys, brought about fear that children have the characteristics and capabilities to be potential murderers thus

---

9 Cited in Worrall, A. (1997: 34) Punishment in the Community: The Future of Criminal Justice

increasing fears about the children within our society, despite this kind of criminal act by children so young being extremely rare.

Media reports that half of all crime is linked to young people under the age of twenty and that the government is going soft on criminals by sending less young people to prison, giving community sentences instead, keeping young criminals on the streets only reinforces those fears despite this not being the case.

Statistics reveal that young people are mainly the victims of crime. However, John Major, the then Prime Minister at the time, said in a statement during that year, that as far as offenders are concerned '*we should understand less and condemn more*'. [10]

But, if we want to ignore risk factors, how can we possibly reduce reoffending?

The Home Secretary during that year made statements stating that '*prison works*' even though statistics on reoffending have refuted these claims. He reinforced the '*tough on crime*' policies.

The Conservative Party tried to win public approval with their overtly punitive approach to justice as opinion polls suggest that

---

10 Bottoms cited in Haines & Drakefield (1998)

there is much public support for such measures, fear of crime again.

The media have played a major part in increasing fears about young people. A headline such as 'Ratboy' about a young one boy offender who has committed multiple crimes denotes human vermin on our streets. Fear that an individual young boy may run amok through our communities destroying everything we have worked hard for does no justice to young people in general yet alone those committing petty criminal acts.

This one wave crime so called *Ratboy* a 14 year old who committed numerous offences and lived rough in a heating duct. Justice workers would argue that if he and received help and had his basic needs met then perhaps he wouldn't have committed the crimes.

The effect these media reports and similar ones had left negative attitudes towards future young offenders which were again felt within the criminal justice as the pressure to 'clean up our streets of human vermin' took hold. The press received the information from the police on this young offender and another 57 persistent young offenders in 1996.

The negative press put pressure on the government which led to Secure Training Centres being introduced by the government for those whom were or were likely to become persistent young offenders. [11]

The media should try to balance out these fears by stating something good that a young person has done with every negative piece to address the problem of fear of crime.

Without knowing the real reasons why young people commit the type of criminal acts they commit we cannot give the individual guidance that they so desperately need to prevent reoffending. Although most crimes are opportunist crimes, not all young people commit the act so what are the determining factors of youth crime? In the so called 'Ratboy' case it was for food and shelter. For others it may be a drug habit or a cry for help from physical or sexual abuse.

Each individual case needs to be looked into before determining the sentence delve deeper than the principles of retributivists and Utilitarianism.

Haines and Drakeford (1998) argue that two dominant and contradictory strands could be detected in public perceptions of young people. The first is linked with envy in that young people have never had it so good.

---

11 Haines & Drakefield (1998:27)

Wearing a pair of expensive trainers costing more than a family of four had to live on for a month only shortly before they were born.

In the second strand, many people view young people with fear and may feel intimidated if walking past a group of young people. Many attitudes are that parents and society are too soft on young people who have no respect or consideration for their elders. [12]

Hopkins stated that it is one of our human rights to go about our everyday lives without fear, yet surveys reveal that most adults are fearful of crime and have been a victim to at least one crime in the last twelve months.

According to many statisticians, the fear of crime was much more of a problem than crime itself.

But an international study suggests that our fears may be justified by the fact that the United Kingdom has the highest crime rates in the industrialised world and as most of that crime is committed by young offenders we have a right to be fearful of them. [13]

---

12 Haines & Drakeford (1998: 3)

13 Hopkins (2001)

Fear of crime has for decades been a problem within our society resulting from much continued bad press and new legislation to combat crime reinforces that fear. Taking away the discretion of the police to give cautions or reprimands to young offenders meant that more and more crime was now being recorded thus immediately distorting figures.

The police were able to give a 'telling off' a number of times to an offender based on their common sense, the age of the child and the pettiness of the act but the government had eroded their power to steer young offenders away from the courts under the (1998) Crime and Disorder Act.

Loader (1996) argued that young people are assumed to be perpetrators of crime and are rarely constructed as victims or as consumers of criminal justice services. Yet much of the attention paid to young 'trouble-makers' may be due to their inexperience and greater likelihood of detection or to the systematic bias of criminal statistics which emphasise visible and easily counted 'street crimes' rather than the hidden crimes of the workplace and the home. [14] The Crime and Disorder Act (1998) together with the government's White Paper *No More Excuses* (1997) published under the Labour Party and personal comments made by Jack Straw attacked the criminal justice system and

---

14 Worrall (1997: 138

reiterated their anti-social themes boasting of a ‘zero’ tolerance of crimes by young offenders and of the excuses behind causes of crime.

These *excuses* are the reasons why a person commits a crime so yet again the long arm of the law will come crashing down on young offenders without addressing the causes of this social problem. Let’s not forget that there was shortly before this Act a general election so the battle had commenced to grab those votes once again.

What better than proposing new legislation beforehand to sway those fearful of crime to vote for a Party willing to control it more?

Once again the government exerted their powers over the criminal justice system by declaring that children of 10 years old, previously excused of criminal charges under the rule of *doli incapax* removed the idea that children of that age were incapable of having the *mens rea* mental reasoning to commit an offence. Once again parent’s duties and responsibilities could now be forced as they would be compelled to attend court with their children and be forced into attending counselling sessions.

The Act also allowed for restorative justice. Restorative justice proposes an element of reparation, which is defined as:

Actions to repair the damage caused by the crime, either materially (at least in part) or symbolically. Usually performed by the offender, in the form of payment or service to the victim, if there was one and the victim wishes it, or to the community. It can include the offender's co-operation in training, counselling and therapy. Reparative actions can also be undertaken for the benefit of the community. Reparation has elements that the offender is showing remorse and willing to make amends by putting something back into the community. [15]

The government stated that they felt there was a need to put their aims on youth justice into statue as the youth justice system has for too long been separate from youth crime prevention.

The six key objectives of the 1998 Act are:

(1) To speed up the time it takes for a young offender to be dealt with to avoid stress to the child and the victim by aiming to halve the time of dealing with a young offender on charge of the offence from 142 days to 71 days. This would enable youth crime prevention measures to be put in place quickly in order that the persistent young offender has less chance of

---

15 Wright (1998)

committing further offences before being administered through the criminal justice system.

(2) The young offender must confront the consequences of their offending behaviour and the effect this has had on their victims, their family and on the community as a whole. The notion behind this is that the offender is less likely to re-offend if the impact of the behaviour is understood by him/her.

(3) By strengthening the factors, which can prevent offending by young people, is likely to reduce offending behaviour through building on factors such as the family, personal, social and/or educational.

(4) The punishment must be proportionate to the crime committed taking into consideration of all matters of the case in order that the offender gets only his 'just deserts' and that victims, the general public and those working within the criminal justice system have faith in the whole process of it administration.

(5) Reparation is encouraged in order that the young offender see the errant of their ways in order that by understanding and taking responsibility for their actions can help the offender modify the behaviour to that of a law abiding citizen.

(6) By providing support and encouragement to parents who lack the skills to help their children through the youth justice process and discourage their children from offending is seen as a key factor in preventing youth crime. [16]

These objectives were to be carried out by established Youth Offending Teams and Reparation Providers where issues, which may be identified as a cause of the criminal behaviour, can be addressed. The government at the time may be seen to be diverting away from the philosophy of punishment through retribution and utilitarianism and adopting a more restorative approach towards young offenders. However, there were early indicators that revealed punitive measures remain both directly and indirectly.

Those punitive measures are also reflected towards the parents of the offending children or to those parents who have failed to ensure that their child attends school on a regular basis.

Other crime prevention measures with a punitive element have been proposed, this time by Merseyside Constabulary in January 2002. They have offered to pilot a scheme, which would see young offenders facing fixed penalties for their acts.

---

16 Crime and Disorder Act 1998 Home Office

The Chief Constable Norman Bettison believes that the system would have an “immediate and tangible impact” as officers would not have to attend court. [17]

They aimed to issue ‘on the spot fines’ to young offenders committing certain minor offences such as graffiti on a bus shelter even proposing to escort them to a cash machine to withdraw the money to pay for the fine. They have not taken into account that not all young people have cash cards and/or money in them at the time they are marched to the cash machine.

Many school children don’t have bank accounts and debit cards so again it would be down to the parents to hand over their card and pin to the child or be escorted to a cash machine themselves with the police officer and their child.

The parents may not have the money to pay the fine or have a cash card. The scheme was frowned upon by many youth justice workers as unworkable and would lead to more young people receiving custodial sentences for non-payment of fines. [18]

---

17 Liverpool Echo January 17th 2002)

18 (Daily Mail January 19th 2002)

CHAPTER 2

Should the welfare of the child be more important than the interests of justice?

This chapter is concerned with the long-standing debate on whether the interests of the child should be paramount rather than the interests of justice. Should we protect the children from the criminal justice system or show them the heavy side of the law as punishment and deterrence? It also identifies some of the risk factors that can cause young people to commit criminal acts and whether the new Orders of the Criminal Justice Act (1998) and its recognition of the risk factors will benefit the welfare of the young offender.

The welfare versus justice debate has been dominant in discussions between youth justice workers, academics, policy makers, community leaders and such for decades. Those in favour of the welfare of the child would generally agree that criminal behaviour is something that the child will grow out of and that it is just a temporary phase and part of growing up. To give a child a criminal record, which will have adverse effects for the rest of their lives is harsh yet worst still, locking up a child for their wrongdoing does not benefit anybody and has a detrimental and lasting effect on the wellbeing of the child and his/her family. Some would also argue that the age of criminal responsibility is set too low by the government at ten years old. [19]

The Children's Society, a national charity in its 'Tough Justice' report called for the age of criminal responsibility to be raised arguing that Britain has one of the lowest ages in Europe at ten years of age for the simple reason that children of this age have not matured enough to know that what they are doing is wrong. Many people would agree and for those who don't some would argue that to put them through the criminal justice system so young is harsh. Those they believe that they should be punished for their acts may believe a sentence from the courts is just what is needed.

Sentences that have been given have been so widespread that concerns have been raised by many commentators.

This sentencing disparity throughout the country resulted in some young offenders receiving much lighter sentences than others for like crimes. This has angered many victims and made a mockery out of the criminal justice system in the press and usually concerns lighter sentences. Also, delays in cases coming to court made it stressful for victims, offenders and

---

19 Steele (2000)

families involved especially if offenders were on remand awaiting sentencing. [20]

Travis (2001) stated that more than 1,000 boys aged 15 and 16 have been remanded in custody in the past eighteen months despite a ten year old government pledge, enshrined in legislation, to end the much criticised practice. [21]

The Reverend Robert Hardy, the Bishop for Prisons (2000) said, "The Church and the Government had a difference of focus over crime and punishment and that the church had to speak for humanity and punishment, irrespective of the government. To condemn 15 and 16 year olds, give them a criminal record and not to do anything for them in a positive way is a disgrace in a society which still claims, in many respects to be a Christian". [22]

The Children's Society said that the conditions some of these children are kept in breach the United Nations convention on the rights of the child, and the Children Act, if they were animals the RSPCA would sue and that it's no use the Home Office telling us how horrible these young criminals are, all that matters is making them better, not worse. [23]

---

20 Travis (2001)
21 Travis (2001)
22 Cited in Steele (2000)
23 Steele (2000)

On the other hand the Orders may enable those children who are in need of the basic care and control to come before welfare services and help the child thus 'nipping the offending in the bud' by ensuring that children take greater responsibility for their actions and including them in the wider community.

The handful of troublesome offenders who create havoc causing misery not only to their victims but the community as a whole should not be allowed to continue with that kind of behaviour. The Orders would now enable the YOT's to try to address the cause of the criminal acts and allow the offender to be made aware of the harm that has been caused and to put right the wrongdoing.

The monitoring of sentencing practices to end sentence disparity across the country and to reduce the numbers of young people being sent to prison reveals that penal sentencing by magistrates has not declined and those sentences have been raised rather than lowered to keep sentencing disparity at bay.

The town of Warrington has a higher than national average of young offenders being sent into a Young Offenders Institute (YOT), the national target is to have less than 30% of cases resulting in a remand in a youth detention centre but Warrington has 45% increase.

Rhona Bradley (2002), Head of the YOT at Warrington praised a Home Office scheme which was launched in April 2002 where 10-17 year olds, who plead guilty to a first offence, depending on the nature of the offence, will be put before a panel of community members and their victims, who wish to participate, to decide their fate. [24] This would likely to benefit the youth as discussions for reparation would mean that the offender before them who has spray painted the victim's garden fence may request that the offender should scrub every bit off him/herself. The offender stays out of court, the victim gets his/her fence back to how it was before the damage and the community may benefit as the offender may not go on to commit further acts of damage within the community.

Whether magistrates in the area adopt these policies though is another matter. Court clerks and magistrates may be unacquainted with the new Orders or perhaps the courts are reluctant to be forced by the government and will sentence in a manner that they see fit. Each individual body of the criminal justice system, the police, probation, the courts, prisons etcetera like to run things their own way using their practices that they have been accustomed to over the years. New legislation may bring about much discontentment and it usually brings about

---

24 Warrington Guardian July (2002)

much change which means disruption within each organisation and some staff just do not like change and will work against it.

It appears that the government's continuity to exert their powers over the judiciary is diminishing any notion of Montesquieu's doctrine of 'separation of powers'. He argued that there was three entirely separate functions of government: legislative, executive and judicial, and that these should be exercised by entirely separate organs, Parliament, the Executive and the Courts and that there should be no overlap of function or personnel otherwise too much power would be concentrated in the hands of one organ, which would lead to tyranny. [25]

During the 1990's the government issued documents to those working within the criminal justice system telling them how to supervise offenders, write reports for the courts, even how to manage the hostels. They drew up national standards with the aim to *strengthen the supervision of offenders, providing punishment and a disciplined programme for offenders, building on the skill and experience and practitioner's and service managers.* [26]

It was not only the courts whose powers were being eroded but also those that the police had enjoyed. The government was

---

25 Hogan (1993)

26 Haines & Drakeford (1998: 27)

publicly informing the police on policy, procedures and practice and how to spend their money and how to set up extra systems to monitor those funds, when forces around the country were already complaining to the government for the lack of funding that they presently had for policing and crime prevention.

The government have exerted their powers again with the introduction of the 1998 Act. As with the Criminal Justice Act (1991) the Crime and Disorder Act (1998) curbs the police powers and the courts' sentencing powers even further. On gaining power, the Labour Party criticised their predecessors handling of the youth justice system through the acknowledgement of an "excuse culture" which had developed because the youth justice system' excused itself for its inefficiency and too often excused the young offenders coming before it'. The new approach was for the government to have more power in the prevention of crime and not place it solely in the hands of the police. [27]

The government today is undoubtedly in more control of crime prevention, practice and procedure of youth justice. The great political philosopher Montesquieu had the notion of the doctrine of 'separation of powers' within the criminal justice system in the

---

27 Button and Loveday (2001)

interests of fairness. It can be said that the government had eroded this notion over the years.

They could also argue that as they not only receive continued criticism for lack of faith in within the criminal justice system and they supply the funds they have every right to decide how those funds are to be spent and to which many people would agree, especially if they fear crime.

Too much power in the hands of the government could result with many more offenders being sentenced to prison with little recourse to appeal as the state has the power over the courts. The human cost of injustices could never be measured even if the heavy financial one can.

The government also exerted their powers even further towards the parents of young offenders by reviving their 1991 policies which required parents to attend court with their children, make them responsible for payment of fines and to bind over the parents of a child under 16 under Section 58 of the Act to ensure that they 'take proper care and exercise proper control over the child' This was strengthened in the 1998 Act with the Parenting Order.

In in May 2002 the media ran a report that the mother of two teenage children was sentenced to prison for two months for allowing her daughters to refrain from school for up to six months at a time. She said that she could not force her daughters to go to school but the court held that she had a duty to ensure her children went to school and she had neglected that duty.

A couple of weeks later The Court of Appeal reduced her sentence but acknowledged that she was right to be sentenced reiterating the earlier courts' decision that she had a duty of care to ensure that her children went to school. The Minister of education said he was delighted with the Court of Appeals' decision not to quash her sentence saying that schools do everything within their power to get children to attend and stay in schools therefore if parents fail in their duty to ensure that their children go and stay in school which is paramount for their education, they should be held responsible. [28]

The Crime and Disorder Act has finally acknowledged that there are certain factors that are lined with criminal behaviour.

The new YOT funding for 2002-2003 takes into account indices of deprivation for the first time. Mark Perfect, the Chief Executive of the Youth Justice Board said, "The new funding formula recognises the clear correlation between deprivation and offending behaviour by young people. [29]

---

28 BBC News 20th May 2002

29 Youth Justice Board News (2002)

Risk Factors Identified

Crime committed by the young is not caused by any particular factor, as young people who have similar backgrounds and live in a similar social and family circumstance may never commit any criminal acts. Opportunity may be the cause of the crime to one person whereas another may not take up the opportunity to commit the act perhaps for fear of being caught.

However, various researchers have identified factors that the young offender is open to which may be the cause of the offending behaviour. These include the following:-

- *Truanting*
- *Current school exclusion*
- *Drug abuse*
- *Alcohol abuse*
- *Other substance abuse*
- *Antisocial peers*
- *Known offender(s) in home*
- *Poor parent/child relations*
- *Poor parental supervision*
- *Referred to mental health service*
- *On at risk register* [30]

---

30 Holdaway, Davidson, Dignan, Hammersley, Hine & Marsh (2001)

Another important risk factor is *'Previous Offending'.* Studies have proved that the more criminal acts that an offender commits, the more likelihood that the offender will re-offend. [31]

The New Orders & Justice

The new Orders may bring more young people into the criminal justice system. The police are now to give reprimands only if the offence is deemed petty and only once to an offender. The reprimand replaces the previous police caution for under 18's and stays record until the child is eighteen. It can be used in court as evidence of previous contact with the police. Should the child commit a further petty offence within two years then the punishment is likely to be much harsher. As the Act also allows for the introduction of secure training centres for children as young as twelve, a child who has committed more than one petty offence could soon find him/her becoming labelled as a persistent offender and possibly risk being sent to a secure unit. [32]

The damage that this can do the child can have detrimental effects that can last a lifetime. Apart from any emotional scarring there is a risk of physical scarring. There were over 200 deaths of young people under the age of twenty one within the last 10 years. [33]

---

31 Murray in Hudson (1994)
32 Steele (2000)

The Children's Charity revealed that there are over 1000 incidents every week of self-harm by young people in prison. [34]

This rate will undoubtedly and unfortunately increase in the future if penal penalties continue. It appears that justice may come at too severe a price than the welfare of the young offender.

Many young offenders who come into the criminal justice system are from the lower classes. Murray said "there is now an underclass of poor, homeless and/or unemployed people with unstable family relationships who are responsible for most of the crime and disorder within our society". [35]

Hudson agrees with this statement but also argues that this is not due to the fact that those from the middle classes do not commit crime, but their crimes are less publicised and offenders are much cleverer at hiding their crimes. [36]

The Orders can have the benefit of addressing young offender's identifiable risks that may cause the crime by referring them to the appropriate person or organisation such as a drug counsellor at the local Alcohol & Drugs Service. (ADS) if the

---

33 BBC News (24th October 2012) Prison Reform Trust warning over youth custody deaths

34 Steele (2000)

35 Murray (1990: 16)

36 Hudson (1994:18)

offender is committing acts of theft for example, to fund a drug habit.

They can enable the offender to see the harm that has been caused by the behaviour through discussion with the YOT team and/or with the victim. They may be able to redeem their criminal act through retribution by putting something back into the community such as conservation work for the benefit of those who live there.

There is the added benefit of a non-penal sentence although if the offender does not participate with the Order a stiffer penalty may be imposed for the breach.

CHAPTER 3

Summary of five of the Orders

The focus of this chapter is a brief summary of five of the Orders under the Criminal Justice Act (1998), to which this book is based upon.

The Action Plan Order aims to challenge offending behaviour and its causes through a programme of interventions. By addressing the problems of the offender and helping him/her through them.

The Order also aims to make offenders take responsibility for their offending behaviour by trying to put things right through reparation either directly with the victim or within their local community. The Order lasts for three months and the offender must be aged between 10 and 17 to be given the Order. It is aimed at those offenders who have committed an offence deemed serious enough to warrant a community sentence.

The Child Safety Order is aimed at children aged 10 years old and under. Curfews can be given if a child of this age is in a public place after 9pm aimed at those children who gather in public places to cause misery and mischief to the local community. They are made by the Magistrates' court upon an application by the local authority and places the child under the supervision of a 'responsible officer' a member of a YOT or a social worker who co-ordinates the Order.

The Order can be made if a child has committed an act where had the child been aged 10 or more would have constituted a criminal offence, or the Order is necessary in order to prevent such an offence. The Order can also be made if a child has breached a Curfew Order even though no criminal offence was committed in the first place. The Orders generally last for three months but can be extended for up to 12 months in certain circumstances.

The Reparation Order contained in the Act attempts to make the offender aware of his/her actions on the victim and if both victim and offender agree, an appropriate form of reparation is provided, if not directly to the victim, reparation can be given to the wider community.

The doctrine of restorative justice has become increasingly popular to victim support groups; those involved within the criminal justice system and academics due to the positive effect on the victim and on the offender themselves.

The Parenting Order requires the parent of a child to attend counselling or guidance sessions provided by a 'responsible officer', a member of a YOT, a social worker or a probation officer to help and support parents for a period of up to three months.

This Order can be given to parents where poor parent skills are recognised or an Anti-Social Order has been issued on the child, where a Child Safety Order has been made, where a Sex Offender Order has been made on the child or if a child breaches School Attendance Order. This order can be made on a parent or guardian of a child aged ten to sixteen who have committed an offence.

The Final Warning can be given to a young offender aged ten to seventeen by the police if they deem the offence is appropriate for a final warning and only if he is/she is aware that they and their parent or guardian must work with the Youth Offending Team (YOT's) and complete a short programme of intervention either at the YOT's office, at home or a central location.

If the offender gets into trouble within two years of the final warning will almost certainly go to straight to court for convicting and sentencing.

A provision within the Act contains a ***Change Programme*** and is seen as an important means of recidivism as many first-time offenders do not go on to commit further offences whilst cautioned by a police officer under the previous cautioning provision.

The Change Programme delivered by the YOT's will put together a behaviour change programme to address the offender's attitude and behaviour, which led to the criminal offence after looking into the young offender's social circumstances.

CHAPTER 4

Review of Previous Work

This chapter is concerned with reviewing the works of others, looking at their aims and objectives, their methods, findings, scope and aims of their work and the problems that they perceived during their research.

A study by Holdaway, Davidson, Dignan, Hammersley, Hine and Marsh of the Research, Development and Statistics Directory, part of the Home Office called *New Strategies to Address Youth Offending* (2001) was carried out to gather information and evaluate the data of the pilot youth offending teams that were set up with the objective reducing criminal behaviour of young offenders. Their report was based on three reports that were written after six, twelve and twenty four month's work and these were all contained in a single document.

In anticipation of the Crime & Disorder Act 1998 the Home Office established nine pilot Youth Offending Teams with the hope of ironing out any problems that may arise from the pilot studies.

Sheffield, Wessex, West London and Wolverhampton were granted the fuller powers than Devon, Luton and Bedfordshire, Lewisham, Sunderland and St. Helens had less powers.

Their Aims & Objectives

The pilot study hoped to ascertain whether the Act could successfully enforce the new Orders without too many problems occurring whilst the pilot study was undertaken and if a systematic approach to establishing practice and procedures could be adopted and deployed on a national level.

Their Methods

The evaluation teams from three universities used various methods to collate and analyse the information, which was to identify patterns that emerged, aid guidance to improve better practice. Methods included discussions with staff, observation and questionnaires.

Scope and Aims of Their Work

The establishment of the YOT's would mean that staff from the police, probation, social services, education and health authorities would unite for the aim of reducing offending behaviour by "nipping it in the bud". (*Home Office 1997)*

The united team would share an office working as a team to put carry out the objectives of the Act. They could also use seconded staff from other agencies that they felt were relevant including housing and youth agencies. The managers of the YOT's would start from scratch using the guidelines laid down by the Home Office. They had roughly three months to set up the new administrative procedures, employ the various staff and train them, put into place and develop the system and practices. Naturally this would result in chaos. Establishing the administrative procedures and evaluating them in time to report on the pilot study with the view of recognising and improving the system for the full Act to be set into place would have certainly placed managers and other staff under immense pressure.

Perceived Problems

The results themselves were expected to be difficult to obtain by the researchers as not all the YOT's were yet established on a nationally. Some were given fuller powers than others and administrative procedures obviously may take longer to set up from area to area. For example, recruiting seconded staff from one area to another could take several days in one area and several weeks in another if ideal candidates are not so easily found in the field of social services, health workers, youth workers, education officers, probation officers and such.

Other Research

Reading of the research by Jean Hine and Anne Celnic at the University of Sheffield in November (2001) called *A One Year*

Reconviction Study of Final Warnings was undertaken in order that reoffending rates of those who had previously given a final warning could be analysed.

Their Aims & Objectives

They aimed to look at reoffending rates of those who had been given a final warning in comparison to those who had been cautioned in 1998. Whereas the final warning automatically triggers off a referral to a YOT, the police caution was a reprimand (a telling off) with no court intervention. The study was carried out as a part of the evaluation of the pilot study by Holdaway et al, (2001). The effect of the final warning on reconviction rates after a one year period was assessed as previous studies such as Kershaw et al (1999) had undertook revealed that over two thirds of first reconvictions occur within twelve months of the original disposal even though previous research is usually based after 24 months of original disposals. [37]

Their Methods

They followed up 856 final warnings that were given and analysed the results and data from an evaluation of the pilot youth offending teams contained in Holloway and others study (2001).

---

37 Hine & Celnick (2001)

They compared data from a sample of 4,718 young offenders between the ages of 10 and 17 across the country who had been cautioned in 1998.

The research methods they used were logistic regression analysis, due the different statistical data which would have affected the results.To obtain data on reconviction they used information from the Police National Computer which records further cautions and warnings as well as current court proceedings.

Aims and Scope of their Research

The old police caution may have been used regularly between forces to offenders on multiple occasions as the police had much discretion as to whether to caution or charge an offender. Now the police are under a legal obligation to give a reprimand or final warning, which automatically triggers off a referral to the YOT.

Whereas a police caution (or two) may have previously deterred one offender who has committed a minor criminal act into reoffending the new final warning system may result in the offender entering the criminal justice system as now police, probation, social services, education and such have become involved perhaps stigmatising the young person as trouble. The offender may appear known now to more than one social agency.

The new final warning could also have the positive effect of ensuring that an offender does not repeat his offending act or go on to commit more serious criminal acts if more than one agency is working together to deal with a variety of social problems.

Whilst extracting the results from the Police National Computer researchers found that it took around eight weeks for the data to appear on the system after a conviction and therefore, some offences that may have been committed between ten to twelve months after the first disposal may not have been entered onto the Police National Computer.

Therefore, reconviction rates can only be used as a general guide as crimes may have been committed by an offender and have been unreported for whatever reason or have been reported but not yet been decided upon.

Also, reconviction rates may be distorted as more criminal acts of the offender that would normally be given a caution for are now being referred to the YOT's. This would cause a rise in the reconviction rates.

If previously an offender received multiple cautions for the criminal acts that were committed and gone unrecorded this could now dramatically increase the statistics.

Other Research

NACRO's (2001) Youth Crime briefing *Lessons From Pilots: a summary of the National Evaluation of the Pilot Youth Offending Teams with emphasis on the piloting process, strategic issues, staffing roles and cultures and the use of the new Orders and interventions.*

Their Aims and Objectives

To evaluate the pilot study of the YOT's that was carried out by Holdaway and others and learn from their findings.

Their Methods

Their methods consisted of evaluating their study in order that their findings could be used to summarise and evaluate report as a whole.

Scope and Aims of their Study

To summarise their work briefly and not as detailed an analysis of the full pilot YOT's where reference is made to refer to report for a full detailed analysis using reference to other relevant NACRO Youth Crime briefings.

Other Research

The research by Jennings in June (2000), *One Year Reconviction Rates,* July (2000) cohort: Research Development and Statistics

Directorate: Home Office was judged on outcomes which have been defined in agreement with the Treasury and recorded in the Home Office's Public Service Agreement (PSA) and contain a number of targets including PSA 10, which requires a five percent reduction of juvenile offences within twelve months of a conviction, reprimand or warning based on the 1997 data.

The Aims and Objectives

To examine the outcomes to assess if the targets that were set are being reached.

Her Methods

She used logistic regression in her evaluation of 12,000 offenders that were cautioned or convicted in the first half of 1997 of which 11,994 records were taken from the Police National Computer on a random basis using a predicted rate based on 1997 statistical data.

Scope and Aims of Her Work

As this was a dry-run before the live PSA target results were produced this is only a pilot study and therefore cannot be 100% reliable. For speed and efficiency the target excludes offenders originally sentenced to custody. The collected data was only a sample and cannot therefore reflect the full, true statistics.

CHAPTER 5

Multi-Agency Partnerships

By looking at the benefits of multi-agency partnerships and disseminating the problems that can arise from their formation may be of some help to organisations. Reference to multi-agency partnerships under the Criminal Justice Act (1998) and the establishment of Youth Offending Teams in particular form the basis of this discussion.

Benefits of Multi-Agency and Partnerships

Multi-agencies and partnerships have many benefits with regard to the following:-

Team working – A team has been described as a group of people; who interact with one another; are psychologically aware of one another; and perceive themselves to be a group. Another definition is a collection of people who share most, if not all the following characteristics:

A definable membership

Group consciousness

A sense of share purpose

Interdependence

Interaction

Ability to act in a unitary manner [38]

Several people pulling together to achieve the same objectives can prove to be more effective than individuals working alone especially if working under the same roof as communication can be quickly passed between all staff. Individuals who are part of a team are less likely to feel alienated increasing job satisfaction and motivation.

Blauner (1964) describes alienation in terms of four dimensions.

1. Powerlessness – a workers lack of control over management policy, immediate work processes, or conditions of employment.

2. Meaninglessness – the inability to see the purpose of work done, or to identify with the total production process or unfinished product.

3. Isolation – not belonging to an integrated work group or to the social work organisation, and not being guided by group norms or behaviour.

---

38 Mullins (1993:168)

4. Self-estrangement – the failure to see work as an end to itself or as a central life issue. Workers experience a depersonalised detachment, and work is seen solely as a means to an end. [39]

Other benefits of working together to reach the same objectives are several unitary minds are better than one. Problems can be discussed, addressed and ironed quickly and more easily.

Formal groups are concerned with the co-ordination of work activities and are created to achieve specific objectives. Specific goals are created by management and rules adopted and behaviour established. Youth Offending Teams are formal groups, which have been deliberately planned by the government to achieve specific organisational objectives – to "nip offending behaviour in the bud".

Monitoring the performance of the group may be achieved more easily as the group members will have their defined roles whilst working together under the same roof to achieve the aims and objectives of the organisation.

Problems that can arise within Multi-Agency Partnerships

---

39 Mullins (1993: 485/6)

Defining staff roles pose problems to organisations. If staff members are unsure of the role that is expected of them they may feel that they are not going to 'fit in' which may result in feelings of isolation and disillusion. Staff members need to know what is expected of them and have the ability to do the job required.

A 'role' is the expected pattern of behaviours associated with members occupying a particular position within the structure of the organisation. If they don't meet the expectations of others in inter-agencies, conflict can also arise.

Some people do not like change to their working patterns and may resist the change at every opportunity. Reasons being that they may not see a need for change, or being accustomed to their previous environment through certain pattern of behaviour and habits any change could jeopardise their comfort and security.

More control over their activities may bring about a sense of loss of freedom in the workplace. Their pay and terms of employment may change much to their disadvantage. Fear of the unknown may be another factor resulting in job dissatisfaction and alienation. Conflict can arise if one or more persons are in disagreement. Conflict is behaviour intended to obstruct the achievement of some persons other goals. [40]

---

40 Mullins (1993: 658)

Schmidt believes that conflict makes some people feel demeaned and defeated. The distance between hierarchy of staff may increase, feelings of suspicion and mistrust may develop and a resistance to work within the team. He argues that conflict can have positive effects. Better ideas may be produced; staff may feel obliged to search for new approaches. The chance for some to test and prove their capabilities, creativity and stimulation of interest may arise and some long standing problems may be brought to the surface.

There may be more than one member of staff whom possesses strong leadership skills, which may cause conflict. Mullins describes leadership in general terms *a relationship through which one person influences the behaviour of other people.* [41]

As each manager within the YOT's would have adopted various styles of leadership during management, which they have used during their course of employment such as the authoritarian, democratic or laissez-faire, it is only natural that the varying styles of management will differ from one local authority area to another and this could reflect in the data collated. If there is more than one manager in the organisation whose managerial styles conflict, then defining and maintaining staff roles, carryout out practice and

---

41 Schmidt in Mullins (1993: 229)

procedures and general organisation of the workplace can be thrown into chaos. Staff may be used to their manager adopting a certain manner, different staff now forming part of the YOT's may not.

The authoritarian style of management is where the manager has total control over all the decision making retaining all the power over the staff. This type of manager may cause friction within the YOT's. The democratic style of managements is centred on sharing the power amongst staff with the group who have a say in how policies and procedures are to be placed. This style of management could cause chaos within the YOT's as each agency may be used to using their own powers and a battle for hierarchy may occur. The laissez-faire style of management allows for capable staff members to make their own decisions without interference from the manager but who will help if the staff members require it. This is the best style of management with a YOT team who will be making decisions with regards to individual young offenders.

Conflict can arise at all levels if the right management style is not adopted and result in job dissatisfaction and alienation forcing individuals to leave that employment. Although individuals may be seconded to work together as a team in the YOT team to reach the same objectives, working similar hours, doing similar work their employment contracts may differ. Thus within the YOT's police, probation, social services, health and education staff are likely to be on different pay scales, different holiday allowances etc. resulting in conflict.

It has long been established that each agency such as the police, probation, social services, health and education have their own set of rules, practices and standards having established these and building on

them over decades. Although they have previously overlapped one another by working in partnerships they have kept their own status, regulations, practices and individual powers by remaining independent of one another. It would be inevitably cause some inefficiency and ineffectiveness to bring individuals together from these agencies and expect teamwork to run smoothly whilst implementing new systems in such a short space of time whilst being monitored by those carrying out the pilot studies on behalf of the government.

CHAPTER 6

Results

The aim of this chapter is to discuss the results of the pilot studies of the Youth Offending Teams and Reparation Providers that were found. Due to the scope and aims of the work and issues that the YOT's faced with policy and practice the results can only give a general idea of whether the Orders are effective in reducing offending behaviour and could be challenged in future years.

The Pilot Study of the Five Orders

By using data of the five Orders that were imposed on young offenders during the 18 months of the pilot study was first collated to give some idea if a particular Order was preferred and used by the YOT's. The results are shown in chart one.

Chart 1

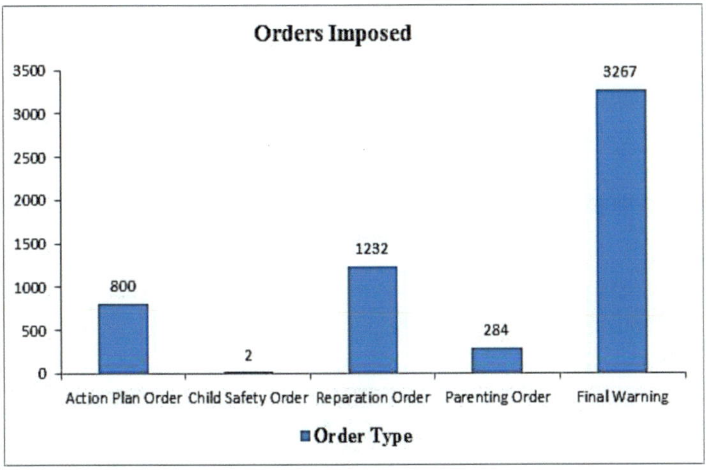

Results

The chart shows that the final warning is imposed approximately two and half times more than the reparation order with the child safety order being used only twice. As the police give the final warning, which triggers a referral to a YOT, the police may either see the offence as trivial and which they may have previously given the old caution for or are reluctant to instigate full criminal proceedings for the welfare and future welfare of the child. It may be that they are unwilling to forego their powers of discretion to prosecute which the government are trying to curb.

Holdaway, and others (1998) in their analysis of offending history of those given the final warning were collated and have been displayed in percentages in chart two.

Chart 2

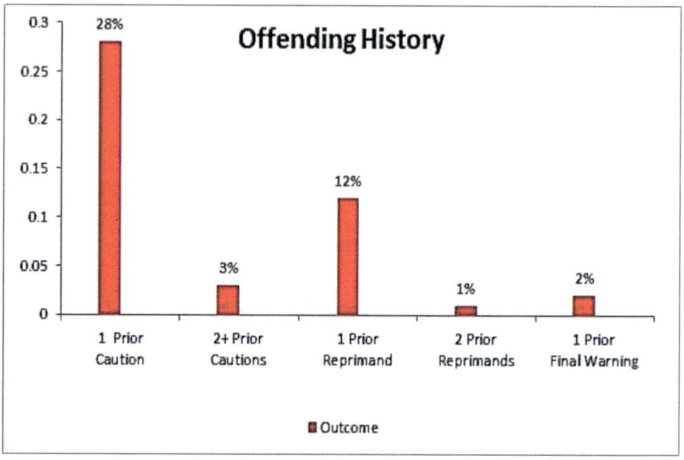

Results

The results reveal that twenty eight percent of young offenders had one previous police caution and therefore referred to the YOT's compared to only one percent having two prior reprimands. This shows that most young offenders may stop offending after two police cautions.

This would suggest not only that police are not are more knowledgeable about young offenders and their likelihood of committing further offences and the long-term harm that a criminal record can have on a young person but that a young offenders usually grow out of crime after a couple are cautions and therefore the new Final Warning was unnecessary.

The types of offence that final warnings were given as shown in chart three were as follows:-

Chart 3

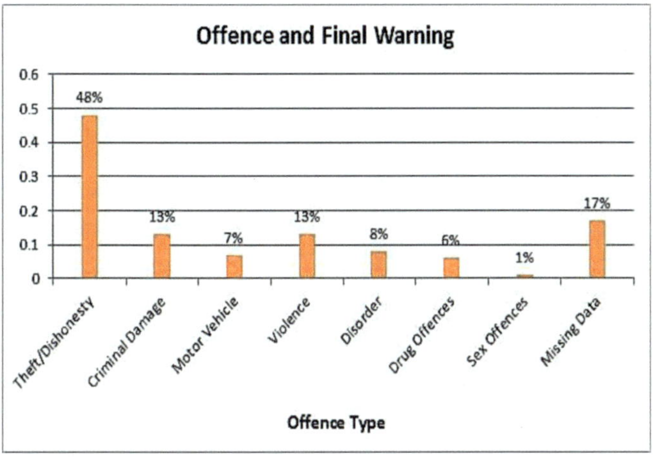

Results

It appears that young people commit more offences of theft and dishonesty and as these offenders were given a final warning and not a heavier penalty we can presume that these offences were of petty theft and dishonesty and not a more serious criminal act.

Final warnings were only given to one percent of young people who had committed sexual offences perhaps as this type of crime warrants a more serious punishment than a final warning and/or and committed less often than other types of offence but we do not know what offences are contained in seventeen percent of missing data.

Gender of Offender

Chart 4

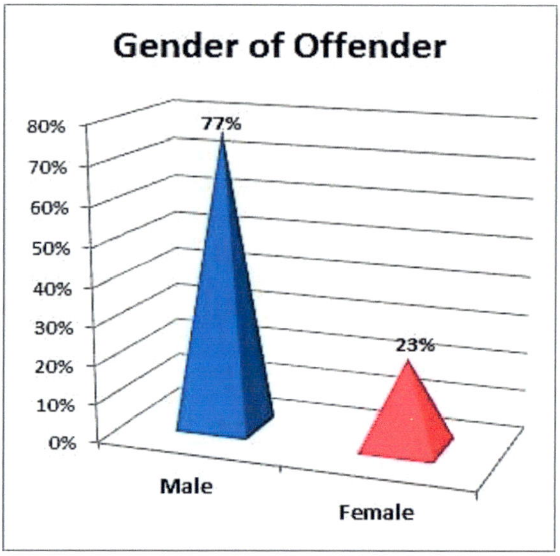

Results

Males were approximately three times more likely to commit offence and/or be given a final warning by police. This either means that females commit less crime or that they are not given the option of the lesser punishment of a final warning.

But, a study by Prime, Liriano & Kinnari revealed that 33% of males that were born in 1953 had a conviction by the time they reached the age of 46 compared to only 9% of females who were born in the same year so perhaps females do commit less crime statistically. [42]

Race of Offender

Table one consists of the race of offenders that were given final warnings from the results derived from the pilot study. [43]

---

42 Prime, Liriano & Kinnari Study (2001)

43 Holloway, S. et al (2001) *New Strategies to Address Youth Offending*

Table 2

Race of Offender	% Given a Final Warning
White	77
Black	10
Asian	4
Other ethnic background	4
No ethnicity recorded	6
Not known	4

Results

Table one shows that white males are the highest race and gender to be given a final warning by the police while other ethnic groups totalling 28%, are less likely to be given the final warning. The results would suggest that either more young white males commit less serious criminal offences or more young offenders from ethnic minorities are not given the lesser penalty of a final warning and sent to the courts instead for sentencing.

Many commenters have shown concern with regards to this matter which grew in since the early 1980's on the high statistical data of black minority groups and females in our prisons. They believe that the typical stereotyping in our society that black minority groups are biologically more inclined to commit crime than whites and that females who commit crime must have a mental defect to go against their presumed feminine characteristics of being mild mannered and passive. Black women face a double jeopardy and are likely to receive stiffer sentences again. [44]

The mean age for young offenders receiving the final warning was 14.5 years and 40% of young offenders lived with both parents. The evidence suggest that there is only a ten percent difference of young offenders being in one-parent families therefore the difference is not high enough to suggest that children from so called *broken homes* are more likely to commit criminal acts.

Action Plan Orders

Of the eight hundred Action Plan Orders that were given during the eighteen months pilot study, again these were given overwhelmingly to white males.

The types of offence that brought about the Action Plan Order are summarised in chart five.

---

44 Maguire, Morgan & Reiner (1997)

Chart 5

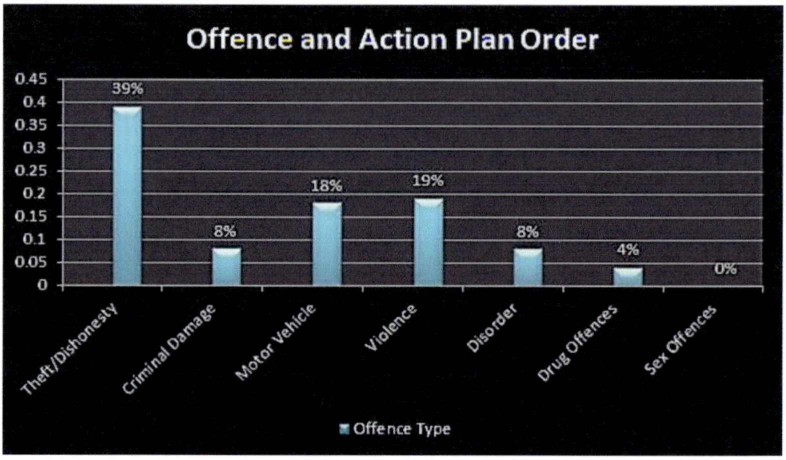

Results

The Action Plan Order was given to thirty nine percent of young people who committed acts of theft and dishonesty. No young offender who committed sexual offences was given the Action Plan Order. This Order was given to those whose criminal acts were seen to be more serious in nature than to warrant a final warning so we can presume that the acts committed were considered more than petty offences by the police.

Out of the forty seven percent of those offenders who were given the Order, twenty three percent had previous sanction. Peer pressure was identified as a high risk factor in sixty six percent of young offenders, truancy was the second highest factor at forty percent and poor parent/child relations at thirty nine percent as highlighted in graph six. Other substance abuse and on the 'at risk' register had the lowest risk factors.

Chart 6

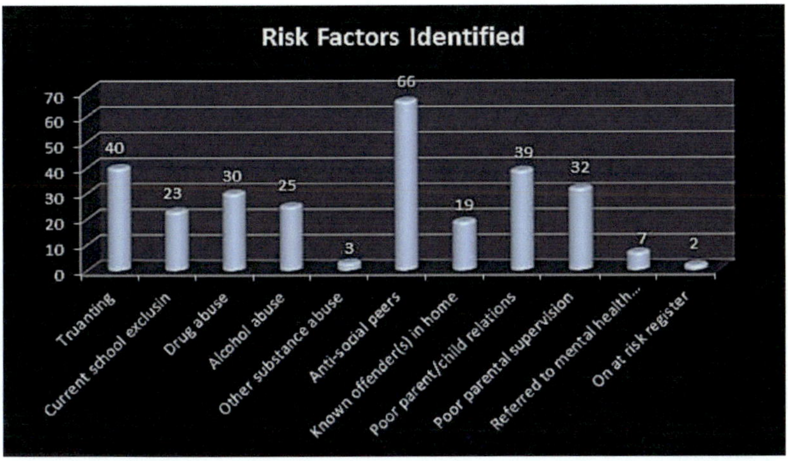

Child Safety Orders

There were only two child safety orders and therefore evaluation was unable to take place of the pilot YOT's. Questions were raised as to why they were not being used to the full extent with regards to procedure of referral and assessment, failings to identify relevant children and actual criteria for a recommendation to the Order. Those evaluating the pilot study closely examined policy and procedure documents and key members of staff were interviewed in order for the answers.

Visiting and asking the various agencies such as the police, housing, education and social services staff was undertaken to ascertain the reasons for evaluation purposes.

The Parenting Order

This Order was given to the parents of 284 young offenders Out of the 279 that were analysed sixty two percent were given to the youth courts following criminal proceedings of the young offender.

Thirty seven percent were made by the education authorities for the failure of the child to attend school regularly and one percent on parents following on from the Child Safety Order. Results illustrated in chart seven.

Chart 7

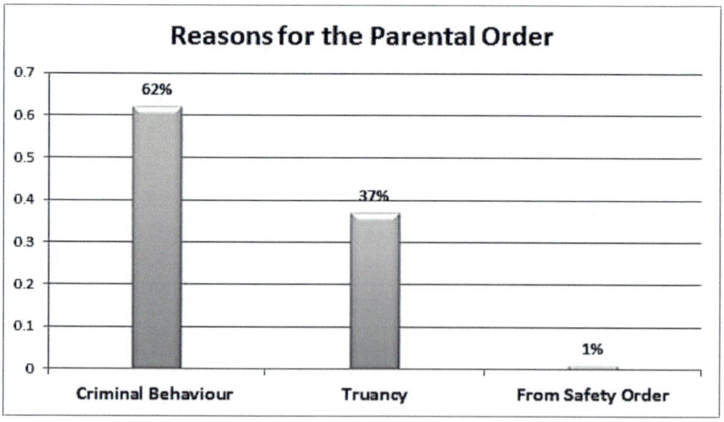

Gender of Parents Involved

Table three illustrates the gender of the parents who were compelled to the Order. The results reveal that more female lone parents were nearly twice as likely to be subjected to the Parenting Order as a lone male parent would. Fathers who were part of the family where both natural parents resided were just over twice as many times to become subject to the Parenting Order. Therefore we can presume that if both parents are living together at the time of the child's criminal act, the father is held more responsible for the child actions. Yet the mother is almost twice as likely to be subjected to the Order as a lone father. We do not know if this is so as he is expected to work if he is a lone parent whilst the lone mother may be expected to stay at home and care for her child. Reason for this need a closer analysis.

Table 3

Household	Women	Men
Lone Parent	53%	30%
Both Natural Parents	23%	47%
Other	24%	23%
Total	100%	100%

Age of Parents

The ages of the parents involved in the study of the Parental Orders widely varied from 28 to 58 years and similarly parents from those children who had committed a criminal act were also various ages as to those parents of children whom committed truancy.

Therefore, no real assessment of age of parents to age of child at time of committing an offence can be made. The mean age of parents subjected to the Order was 38 for females and 40 for males based on the ages that were made available as not all the data was present so can only be used as a general guide.

Chart eight reveals that fifty seven percent of children on the Criminal Order were at risk of committing crime through truancy.

Poor supervision of their children by parents was thirty three percent. Offending peers at thirty two percent. Poor relationship with one or both parents stood at twenty percent. Truanting children are more likely to commit crime of petty theft and dishonesty presumably during the time of the truanting as this is the offence most committed and perhaps whilst truanting with peers.

Chart 8

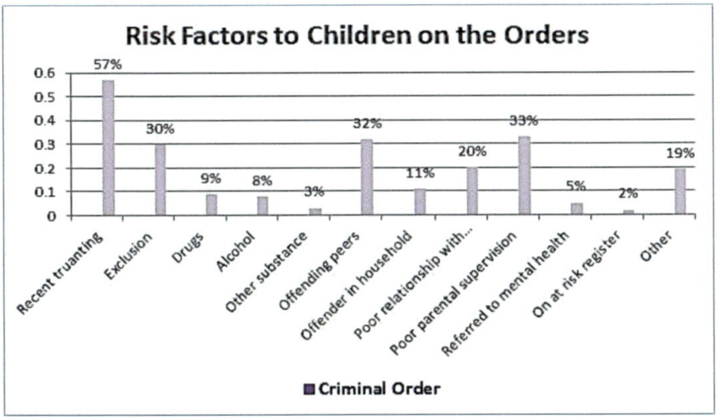

The Reparation Order

This order was given to 1,232 young offenders. The YOT's favour this Order as well as the offenders themselves as most of the participants believed that making amends for the harm that had been done by is more just.

Restorative measures that were developed consisted of support and assistance to the victim and putting in place measures that would be beneficial to the community as a whole such as cleaning graffiti from walls.

Members of the panel would consist of unpaid volunteers from the general public recruited by the YOT's and a member of the YOT along with the victim and the offender's parents to draw up a plan which would help to repair the damage that the offender had done when committing his act This enabled the YOT and the victim to let it be known the impact that the offence had had on others and to hopefully see this and not commit another offence again.

Gender of Offenders

Eighty five percent of the offenders were male and fifteen percent were female as displayed in pie chart one.

Pie Chart 1

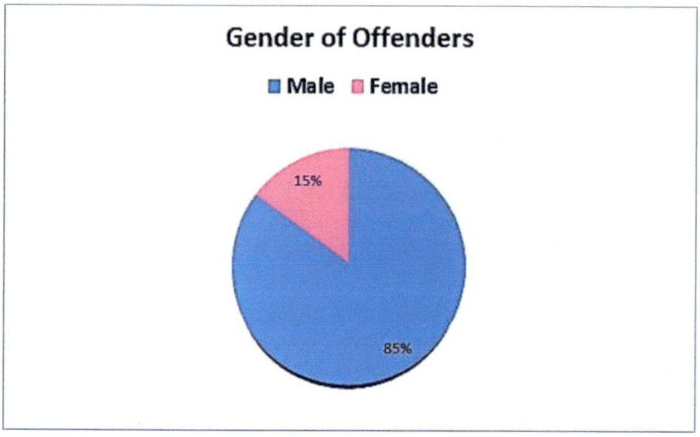

Ethnicity of Offenders

The overwhelming majority of offenders who were given the Reparation Order are white. Nine percent of offenders did not want to state their race for whatever reason. Pie chart two illustrates the results of the ethnic origin of the offenders.

Pie Chart 2

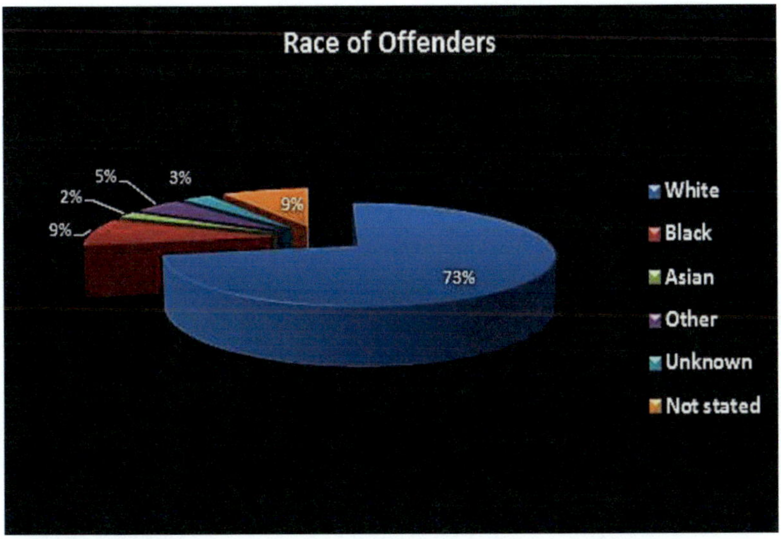

Age of Offenders

The mean age of offenders who were given the Reparation Order was 14.3 years.

Risk Factors Identified

Anti-social peers was a high risk factor at sixty three percent with poor parent relations being next highest at twenty nine percent with truanting coming after that at twenty six percent and poor parental supervision at twenty five percent as depicted in table four.

Table 4

Known Risk Factor	% At Risk
Truanting	26%
Current School Exclusion	19%
Drug Abuse	16%
Alcohol Abuse	15%
Other Substance Abuse	2%
Antisocial Peers	63%
Known Offender(s) in Home	20%
Poor Parent/Child Relations	29%
Poor Parental Supervision	25%
Referred to Mental Health Service	5%
On at Risk Register	4%

Offence and Reparation Order

Chart nine illustrates the offence for which the young offender was given the Reparation Order.

Chart 9

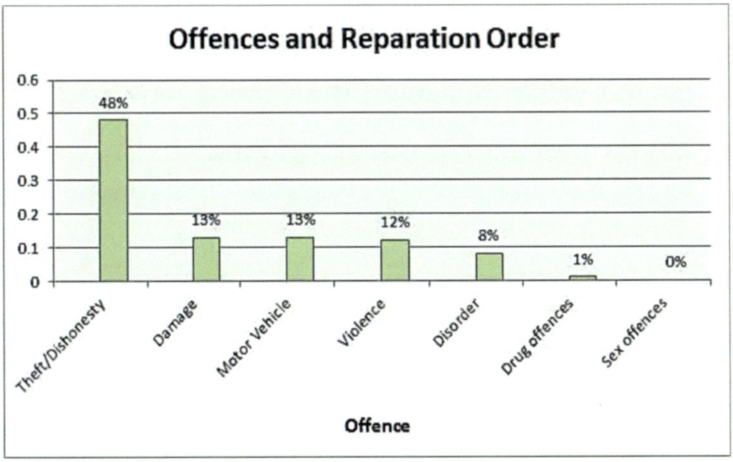

Results

The results reveal that young offenders were given Reparation Orders for the offence of theft and dishonesty in forty eight percent of the cases. As other graphs have shown that theft and dishonesty is the offence committed the most by young people this order seem more appropriate in addressing the offenders behaviour and repaying back some good to the victim or the community.

With regards to staffing the YOT's there were concerns about the selection of staff as some members had difficulty in doing their da-to-day tasks due to inadequate skills that the policies require. For example, if a member is given a job of inputting details into a computer and is not familiar with the particular computer package then they may not be suitable for the job especially if they have no enthusiasm to learn. Members of the team who were given the option to be seconded to the YOT's were more positive about the roles they played within the team than those who had been given no option. Some members were considered totally unsuitable for the role.

Some of the opinions of the attitudes of staff were assessed by the pilot team and depicted in table five. [45]

---

45 Holdaway, S. Davidson, N. Dignan, J. Hammersley, R. Hine J. and Marsh, P (2001) Research, Development and Statistics Directorate: Home Office New Strategies to Address Youth Offending.

Table 5

Statement	% Agreed
Positives Points	
Like working in YOT	81%
See new law as significant change	82%
Like people I work with	82%
Mix of workers stimulating	79%
Like working with young offender	86%
Approve of single reprimand	47%
Team has shared view of work	42%
Negative Points	
Act contains contradictions	58%
Time wasted through lack of support staff	44%
Team members not informed/consulted enough	36%
Too little attention to young offenders	36%

The results reveal most members of the team enjoyed working within it and that the new law did bring about a significant change.

There did appear to be a high percentage of staff who thought that the new Act did contain contradictions therefore there may have been confusion on which Order was more appropriate to use. Future analysis may throw up completely different results as to the Order which is more favoured by the YOT's. A major concern from these findings is that less than half of team members felt that the team had a shared view of work. This means that they may not be working together to carry out the objectives of the government. It was noted that there were tensions between staff that arose due to increased workload. The fact that some members of the team were unsure of exactly what there were there to do had caused some tension.

Some members of the team asked their old managers for guidance rather than the manager within their team. This would appear that either:

1. That the manager was unapproachable.

2. The manager did not know his role within the YOT team.

3. Staff member was too embarrassed to ask in case the manager thought the member was incapable doing the job and therefore jeopardise any their job or future promotion.

4. Some members of staff were just suited to the post in the first place.

Chart ten shows opinions of staff within the YOT's.

Chart 10

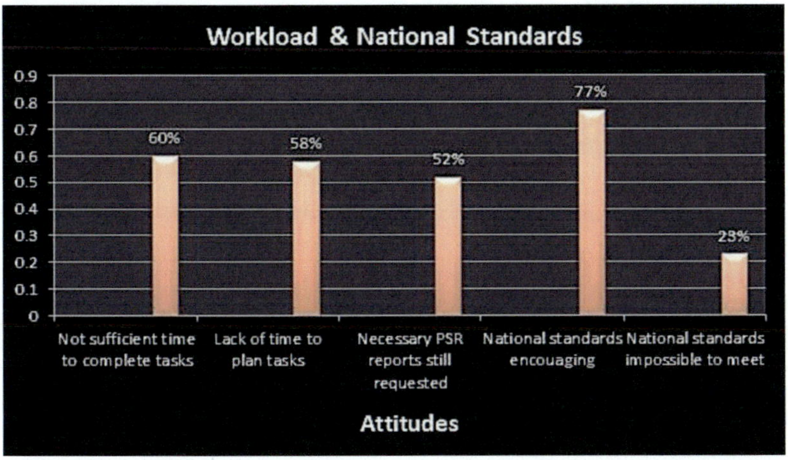

Results

The chart shows that the percentage of staff who was concerned with their workload is significantly high at sixty percent and that basically they felt that they were overworked. They obviously believed that they were thrown in at the deep end by not having enough time to complete their tasks. If some staff members do believe that they can't meet their targets they may leave their position as they may tend to feel that they are unsuitable.

Overview of the Findings from the Pilot Study

It appears from the data that four of the Orders that are given are given to young white males.

The offence type that rated the highest from all four Orders was theft and dishonesty. Truanting, poor parenting and peer pressure were high risk factors for young offenders to commit crimes.

The One Year Reconviction Study of Final Warnings

Table 6

	Given Cautions	**Final Warnings**
Number of cases in follow up analysis	4,718	856
Percentage reconvicted within 12 months	21%	27%

Table six reveals that although the number of cases in the follow up analysis is much higher at 4,741 for those who had a previous caution the reconviction rate was lower than the 856 cases for those who had a previous warning and therefore subsequently referred to a YOT team and undertake a programme of change. [46]

46 Hine, J. & Celnick, A. (2001) *A One Year Reconviction Study of Final Warnings University of Sheffield*

Chart 11

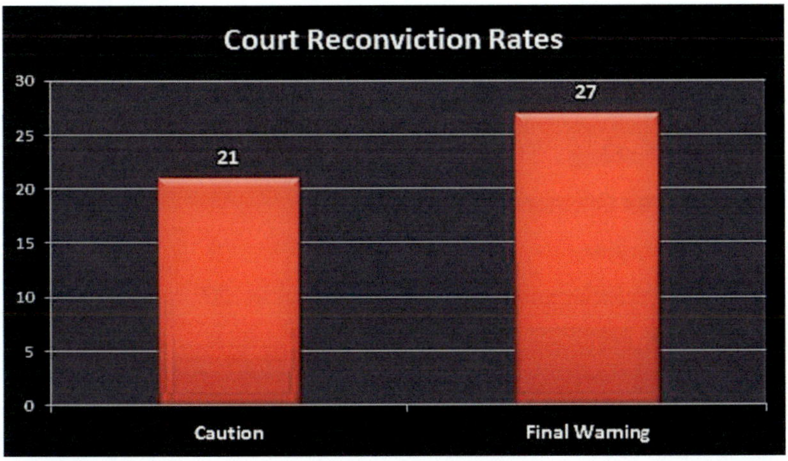

Chart eleven reveals that more than a quarter of young offenders were reconvicted by the court within twelve months of given a final warning compared to twenty one percent whom had previously been given a caution.

Table seven reflects the results of the reconviction offence after a previous caution or final warning.

Theft and handling are the offences which rate the highest at 38% and 37% respectively which means that young offender may be likely to commit the same type of offence that they were previously reprimanded for. Violence at 21% respectively is quite disturbing as it means that some young offenders go on to commit violence against the person, a much more serious offence than petty theft or dishonesty.

Table 7

Offence	Caution %	Final Warning %
Violence	15	21
Sex Offences	1	1
Burglary	9	9
Theft/Handling	38	37
Drugs	7	9
Fraud/Deception	9	3
Criminal Damage	7	12
Other	14	10

Table eight identifies the relationship between risk factors and further criminal acts committed by the offender. [47]

47 Hine, J. & Celnick, A. (2001) *A One Year Reconviction Study of Final Warnings University of Sheffield*

Table 8

Risk Factor	Number Assessed	% Further Crimes
School Exclusion	64	50
Truanting	172	43
Poor Parent/Child Relationship	145	41
Poor Parental Supervision	124	43
Known Offender in Household	90	37
At Risk Register	10	40
Drug Abuse	88	43
Alcohol Abuse	64	34
Other Substance Abuse	17	41
Anti-Social Peers	356	33
Referred Mental Health	38	37

Overview of the Findings of the One Year Reconviction Study

Truanting and poor parenting appear to be high risk factors for young people to re-offend.

NACRO's (2001) Youth Crime Briefing *Lessons from Pilots: a summary of the National Evaluation of the Pilot Youth Offending Teams with emphasis on the piloting process, strategic issues, staffing roles and cultures and the use of the new Orders and interventions was summarised as follows:-*

Strategic Issues

NACRO acknowledged the importance of the steering group in relation to inter-agency work that the pilots had undertaken and that budget concerns were problematic as budgets were based after consultations with local police and the chief executive of local councils taking in factors such as local crime patterns to ascertain each YOT's budget.

Trying to establish an accurate cost of crime was not an easy task for auditors as much of the data that was collected from community partnerships lacked relevant information to extract a figure for costing.

Problems arose due to delegated authority to 'community safety officers' as many lacked the required knowledge and training of community safety to pass on for the audit. There were also wide variations in understanding became a problem between the partnerships as there were wide variations the terms of the various issues involved in the process and were therefore interpreted differently.

A Home Office study based on pilot schemes to test the implementation of the Crime & Disorder Act through Pathfinder Sites to develop crime strategies stated:

"Everyone in the Pathfinder partnerships agrees that the CDA is a big step forward in the field of community safety and crime reduction. They each welcome the statutory footing that previous voluntary arrangements had sought to achieve. It has they argue been easier to convince key players of the need for their involvement in the process" [48]

Staffing Roles and Cultures

The introduction of the YOT's left many existing youth justice workers and social services staff feeling demoralised and underestimated by the shaking-up of the youth justice system. The pilot teams acknowledged that there was tension between staff members from the various agencies initially but working relations got better over time. But, tensions got the better of some staff members who quit their new posts. The lack of time to get used to the new computer system to put into practice the new procedures was felt reverberated throughout the country. Five percent of staff who seconded to the YOT's from education had left, 3% of social services, 1% of police and health. None of the probation staff had left. [49] Either probation staff are more adaptable to change or the right candidates were sent to the posts!

The Use of the New Orders & Interventions

---

48 Button & Loveday (2001: 64)

49 NACRO

The change in working patterns was seen as challenging for many staff members which perhaps suggests that they may have been unsuitable for the job in the first place as some people may find it too hard to adapt or are unwilling to change.

No typical pattern had emerged nationally as the type of Order that was given to offenders differed from area to area. Also, the report noted a 12% increase of custodial sentences by the courts within the first year of the new Orders being implemented. [50]

It appears that justice is still prevailing over welfare of the young offender!

One Year Reconviction Rates

The research by Jennings undertaken in June (2000), called *One Year Reconviction Rates, July 2000* cohort Research Development and Statistics Directorate: Home Office was judged on outcomes which have been defined in agreement with the Treasury and recorded in the Home Office's Public Service Agreement (PSA), and contain a number of expected targets. Chart twelve shows the reconviction rates against the predicted rate including adjustments.

Chart 12

---

50 NACRO

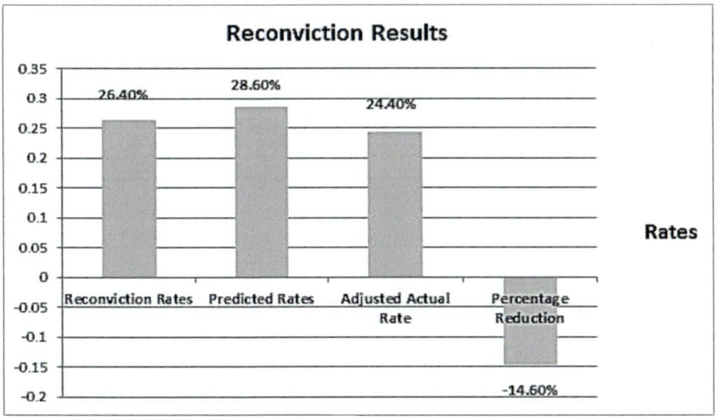

Due to the rushing up of justice which was detailed in the Criminal Justice Act 1998 which did not apply to the results of the data collated from the 1997 data an adjusted rate was used which took into consideration these indices.

The results show that the reconviction rate at 26.4% is marginally lower than the predicted rate of 28.6%. Taking into account the rapid speeding up of justice, the actual rate was 24.4 revealing a minus 14.6% reduction.

Table 9

	First half of 1997	**July 1999**	**July 2000**
Number of Reprimands		209 (3.4%)	5,478 (49.6%)
Number of Final Warnings		95 (1.5%)	1,924 (17.4%)
Number of Cautions	7,528 (63.6%)	3,271 (53.1%)	874 (7.9%)
Number of Convictions	4,306 (36.4%)	2,583 (42.0%)	2,780 (25.1%)
Total	**11.834**	**6,158**	**11.056**

Table nine reveals that figures for July 1999 have been added to take into account the indices that the new disposals were only available to the police in that year in selected areas only. [51]

The use of police cautions has fallen dramatically from the first half of 1997. Sixty three point six percent were given during that time, reducing to 53.1% shortly after the new Final Warning Order was implemented and alarmingly the number of cautions given in July 2000 was down to 7.9% which means that more young offenders are receiving stiffer penalties.

---

51 Jennings, D. June(2000), *One Year Reconviction Rates, July 2000 Cohort Research Development and Statistics Directorate*: Home Office

The data also reveals that there is an increasing use of the number of final warnings given from 95 in July 1999 to 1,924 a year later. The results depict that in the first half of 1999, the percentage of the number of convictions was 36.4% showing an increase to 42.0% in July 1999 but a drop to 25.1% in July 2000.

The report also stated that the cohort revealed data that reflected an increase in the number of offenders with no previous convictions. This may be due to the fact of the final warning Order is bringing more young people to the attention of the authorities. More females with no previous convictions are now also being brought into the system. The future impact that this will have on have yet to be felt.

Pie chart three shows that the reconviction rate for male offenders was 29.5% and 17.6% for females. Related studies reveal that males comprise two thirds of young offenders yet this result shows that female offending rates are increasing nearly twice as fast as males.

Pie Chart 3

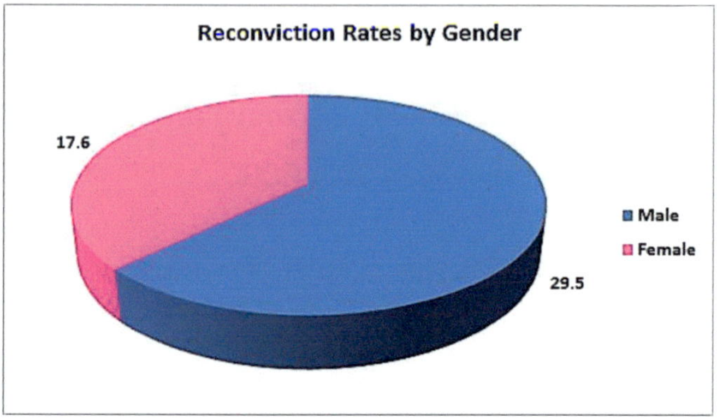

Table ten gives data of the breakdown of the offence type for males and females which reveal that 'other' offences not stated in the table were the highest for males and females. [52]

Theft for males scored high as did criminal damage for females. Robbery offences were the lowest reconviction offence for males and drug offences for females. As we do not know what the *other* offences are we cannot make any presumptions from the findings.

---

52 Jennings, D. June (2000), *One Year Reconviction Rates, July 2000 Cohort Research Development and Statistics Directorate*: Home Office

Table 10

Reconviction Offence	Male	Female
Violence	22.1	17.5
Sexual	19.2	N/A
Burglary	21.8	15.1
Robbery	14.6	16.7
Theft	22.9	12.2
Fraud/Forgery	18.6	13.9
Criminal Damage	22.1	19.7
Drugs	21.4	9.4
Other	43.0	29.5
All Offences	29.5	17.6

The study revealed that the reconviction rate exceeded the predicted rate by 14.6% but there was an increase of reprimands and final warnings, which had the lowest reconviction rates again suggesting that a reprimand or warning is enough for many offenders in preventing them to commit further crimes in the future.

To double check the results, the Offenders and Correction Unit (OCU) asked for data from the Crime and Criminal Justice Unit which collected the results from the courts as well as obtaining statistics from the Youth Justice Board (YJB) collected from the YOT's. Some of the data taken from the NPC of reprimands and final warnings conflicted with that taken from the YJB and the courts. October to December 2000 data was analysed to check for consistency. The results are shown in table eleven.

Table 11

	July 2000	Oct/Dec 2000
Number of Reprimands	5,478 (49.6%)	15,037 (55.0%)
Number of Final Warnings	1,924 (17.4%)	5,042 (18.5%)
Number of Cautions	874 (7.9%)	1,425 (5.2%)
Number of Convictions	2,780 (25.1%)	5,814 (21.3%)
Totals	**11,056**	**27,318**

The results reveal that the percentage was higher for young offenders who were given reprimands and final warnings during October - December than those from data contained from July 2000. There was an increase in the percentages for cautions and convictions from the July 2000 data.

CHAPTER 7

Conclusion

This chapter concludes briefly the five Orders and assesses whether the new legislation can really work.

The Final Warning

The use of the final warning is increasing which more young people are coming into the criminal justice system which will only make the crime rate statistics in the UK look as if they are increasing at a rapid level annually from now on. The impact that this have on *'fear of crime'* will be immense. Britain may also be deemed as *crime ridden* by other countries impacting the economy as tourists may be put off coming to the UK and spending money here. Reconviction rates are also increasing. This may be because now that a young offender is labelled a criminal they continue to act as one as discovered through the 'self-fulfilling prophecy. There were 1,924 young offenders who were given the final warning in July 2000 and 23.9% of these offenders were reconvicted. [53]

In 2001 the figures rose to 3,267 with 46% having at least one prior caution, reprimand or final warning. [54]

---

53 Jennings, D. June (2000), One Year Reconviction Rates, July 2000 cohort Research Development and Statistics Directorate: Home Office.

The Action Plan Order

Jennings found that that out of the 313 young offenders who were subjected to the action plan Order, 51.8% were reconvicted. There were 800 action plan Orders given in the pilot study that was carried out by Holdaway et al in 2001. This Order may reveal much greater improved results in the future as they benefit the offender and the community as a whole by looking at risk factors and ways to address them.

The Child Safety Order

There were no recorded cases of the child safety Order in Jennings 2000 study and only two in Holdaway and others study therefore, reconviction rates were unobtainable and reoffending rates could not be established. Safety of our children is paramount therefore this Order may stay and be used for many years.

The Reparation Order

Jennings (2000) sample study revealed that of the 340 young offenders subject to the Order, 44.7% reoffended. There are no reconviction rates on the pilot study by Holdaway et al from the

---

54 Simon Holdaway, Norman Davidson, Jim Dignan, Richard Hammersley, Jean Hine and Peter Marsh (2001) Research, Development and Statistical Directorate, part of the Home Office called New Strategies to Address Youth Offending.

1,232 young offenders who were subject to the Order. This Order will undoubtedly work and is showing promising signs so far.

The Parenting Order

There were 284 parenting Orders in the Holdaway et al (2001) pilot study and none recorded in Jennings (2001) study therefore reconviction rates could not be assessed. At the present time I cannot assess if one Order is proving to be more effective than another as there was insufficient evidence from research carried out to this date (2002).

Although the pilot study revealed that the reconviction rate was 21% with a previous caution and 28% with a final warning this could be down to the fact that more young offenders are entering the system because of the Orders.

The fact that insufficient time had been set for the policies to be implemented by the police and the courts as well as the YOT's place flaws in the data. Jennings reconviction study resulted in reoffending rates lower than that which have been predicted but, Jennings study was completed using a very small sample and therefore are unreliable in assessing if one Order is more effective in reducing reoffending.

Further studies should continue on the other Orders so that data can be analysed on a regular basis to assess whether any of the

Orders are proving effective in reducing reoffending rates as one year's research with much unrecorded data can only be used possible indicators at the present time. There is much improvement to be had within the youth offending teams. There is sufficient evidence to suggest that the creation of the Youth Offending Teams and Reparation Providers brought about significant problems. These arose due to the seconded staff within the YOT's and those providing the reparation procedures which were to be in place in too short a time from scratch. The amount of time that was allowed in setting up the procedures and producing outcomes for the pilot study caused problems in itself with uncertainty about what exactly what staff members set to do. The pilot study revealed that the average training was just three days.

The recruitment of all future staff should take into account the necessary skills that are required for the posts to ensure that the right candidates are selected. All prospective candidates should have the capability to cope with change. To assess whether candidates are suitable managers could ask questions at the interview stage which reflect their ability in an indirect way, in order that the interviewee does not try to answer the questions in a manner that the interviewer expects from them. With the YOT teams some seconded staff did not have the option of whether they wanted to be part of the YOT team an interview with the appropriate questions may have identified this. This would have prevented some staff from leaving the post putting the existing staff under even more pressure to implement and deliver the government's objectives.

Personality traits could be used to assess whether a person is suitable and has the necessary attitude to change to become part of a 'dream team' such as Eysenck's theory of personality. His theory was based on four personality types based on the ancient Greeks. He devised a technique known as factor analysis in identifying basic aspects of personality derived from answers to his questions on personality. The results of this were categorised to phlegmatic, choleric, sanguine and melancholic and assessed if a person was extrovert or introvert and were based on stable and unstable personalities. The choleric extrovert had a changeable personality and therefore would be adaptable to change. Those deemed to possess personalities from the sanguine type are considered extroverts and deemed to possess leadership skills using Eysenck's theory of personality.

Prospective employees should always be recruited by internal YOT managers and not by the agencies where they are currently employed due to the different skills that may be required and secondment should always be voluntary and not forced by the agencies where they currently work.

The recruitment of managers should involve an assessment of the type of leadership skills that the prospective manager adopts. Where there is more than one manager within the team, managers should be employed who adopt the laissez-faire style in order to reduce conflict. Managers who adopt different styles from one another can cause chaos within a team. The authoritarian style of leadership should be favoured if there is only one manager in charge of staff within the team for containment of power to implement procedures and reducing conflict.

Existing staff members should have their roles clearly defined ensuring that any target outcomes are achievable in a given time. This is imperative if pressure is to be alleviated and for staff to remain committed in their work. They should also be rewarded through praise and an inexpensive gratitude given on a regular basis in recognition for their dedication and commitment. (e.g. a packet of Maltesers, or a pat on the back with the words 'well done, you're doing a great job' goes a long way!)

The government should allow sufficient time for the recruitment of managers and sufficient time for those managers to set up new systems of practice and procedures whenever there is a change in policy before they recruit suitable staff. Placing too much pressure and staff during the initial stages could result in job dissatisfaction and a distortion in the results due to being pressurised to produce the results that may be required from them.

NACRO's (2001) study of the YOT's noticed a 10% overall fall in recruiting staff during the pilot studies therefore, providing clear evidence of job dissatisfaction which may have been caused through neglect or one or more of the above. Ten per cent is quite a high percentage and obviously creates chaos. A multi-agency team need 100% content staff to successfully deliver.

Magistrates' clerks should also be given personality trait tests as magistrates' may tend to be influenced by the clerks due to their knowledge and expertise in dealing with young offenders and the type of case that they are charged with and sentence accordingly. They should be made aware of the Orders and kept up to date with results to ensure that they are not sending young offenders to prison unnecessarily.

Prospective police officers should be recruited who possess not only the ability to carry out the required tasks but the ability to change their attitude in line with each elected governments' new policies.

Those from ethnic minorities have proven to be victims of the criminal justice system and continued measures should be monitored to assess if sentencing attitudes are changing from sentencing white nationals per 1,000 young offenders to those from ethnic minority groups. Recruiting more seconded staff to the YOT's may reduce numbers being sent to the courts in the first place. Also, if more magistrates were recruited from ethnic minority groups this may help to reduce the number of offenders receiving penal sentences.

The government should try to state as far as possible their policies with regards to future funding for the Youth Offending Teams to reassure staff within the teams that their work will continue not only for their reassurance that their jobs are safe but to ensure that their efforts are being recognised as only time will tell if the Orders are proving to be effective in reducing reoffending rates and a reasonable budget should be assessed. But the question remains - *Can it really work and* if so *at what price?*

REFERENCES

Association of Chief Officers of Probation (1993) *Social Circumstance of Younger Offenders under Supervision:* Lancaster University.

Audit Commission (1996) *Misspent Youth London:* Audit Commission.

Button & Loveday (2001) CJS15: *Crime Prevention:* University of Portsmouth.

Crime and Disorder Act (1998) *Youth Justice: The Statutory Principal Aim of Preventing Offending by Children and Young People:* The Home Office.

Farrington, D. (1994) *Human Development and Criminal Careers* in Maguire, M. et al *The Oxford Handbook of Criminology.*

Haines, K. & Drakeford, M. (1998) *Young People and Youth Justice:* MacMillan Press.

Hayes, N. & Orrell, S. (1997) *Psychology: An Introduction:* Longman, New York.

Hine, J. & Celnick, A. (2001) *a One Year Reconviction Study of Final Warnings:* University of Sheffield.

Hogan, G. (1993) *Nutshells: Constitutional & Administrative Law* Third Edition: Sweet & Maxwell.

Holdaway, S, Davidson, N, Dignan, J, Hammersley, R, Hine, J and Marsh, p. (2001) Research, Development and Statistics Directorate: Home Office *New Strategies to Address Youth Offending.*

Home Office (1997) *No More Excuses – A New Approach to Tackling Youth Crime.*

Hopkins, N. Guardian Unlimited 23rd February (2001) *Scared of Being Scared Policing Crime.*

Hudson, B. (1994) *Penal Policy and Social Justice:* MacMillan Press.

Jennings, D. June (2000) *One Year Reconviction Rates,* July 2000 Cohort: Research Development and Statistics Directorate: Home Office.

Leishmann, F, Loveday, B & Savage, S. P. (1996) *Core Issues in Policing:* Longman.

Morgan Report (1991) *Safer Communities* RDS Occasional Paper No. 69: The Home Office.

Maguire, M, Morgan, R & Reiner, R. (1997) *The Oxford Handbook of Criminology* Second Edition: Oxford University Press.

Munice, J. & McLaughlin, E. (1996) *The Problem of Crime:* Sage Publications.

Mullins, L. J. (1993) *Management & Organisational Behaviour* Third Edition: Pitman.

Nash, M. (1999) *Police, Probation & Protecting the Public:* Blackstone Press Ltd.

NACRO's (2001) Youth Crime Briefing *Lessons from the Pilots: a summary of the National Evaluation of the Pilot Youth Offending Teams with emphasis on the piloting process, strategic issues, staffing roles and cultures and the use of the new Orders and interventions.*

Prime, J, White, S, Liriano, S. & Patel, K. (2001) *Criminal Careers of Those Born Between 1953 and 1978* Home Office Statistical Bulletin 4.01 London : HMSO.

Steele, L. Guardian Unlimited 24th November (2000) *End Jail for Under 18's:* The Children's Society.

Stockdale, E. & Casale, S. (1992) *Criminal Justice Under Stress:* Blackstone Press.

Travis, A. Guardian Unlimited 3rd January (2001) *Number of Boys held on Remand Doubles:* Home Affairs Editor.

Twigg, Dr. L. & Moon, Prof. G. CJS5: *Research Methods and Research Management:* University of Portsmouth.

Warrington Guardian July (2002).

Worrall, A. (1997) *Punishment in the Community: The Future of Criminal Justice:* Longman.

Youth Justice Board News March (2002) *Preventing Youth Offending* Travis: Guardian Unlimited 3rd January (2001).

Youth Justice Board.

The Youth Court (2001) *The Changing Culture of the Youth Court, Good Practice Guide:* Home Office.

Made in the USA
Las Vegas, NV
03 November 2026

57424071R00067